FROM COBBETT TO THE CHARTISTS

HISTORY IN THE MAKING

GENERAL EDITOR: *Dona Torr*

FROM COBBETT TO THE CHARTISTS

NINETEENTH CENTURY VOL. 1
1815 – 1848

Extracts from contemporary sources edited by
MAX MORRIS

LAWRENCE & WISHART
LONDON

First published 1948
Second edition 1951

Printed in Great Britain

CONTENTS

PART TWO

TRADE UNION ACTION AND THEORY, 1824–38

PART THREE

IN THE VILLAGE, 1815–42

PART FOUR

THE STRUGGLE FOR POLITICAL AND SOCIAL RIGHTS, 1830–40

PART FIVE

INDUSTRIAL AND POLITICAL ACTION, 1840–8

A) Chartism Reorganised

PART SIX

PRODUCERS AND CONSUMERS

PART SEVEN

THE STRUGGLE FOR FREE THOUGHT

PART EIGHT

INTERNATIONALISM IN THE BRITISH WORKING–CLASS MOVEMENT

ACKNOWLEDGMENTS

OUR thanks are due to the various publishers who have kindly given permission to quote from each of the following works:

The Life of Holyoake (Messrs. Ernest Benn); *Condition of the Working Class in England in 1844*, F. Engels (Messrs. George Allen and Unwin); *The Builders' History* (1923), R. W. Postgate (The National Federation of Building Trades Operatives); *Joseph Arch: The Story of His Life, told by Himself* (*1898*), (Messrs. Hutchinson & Co.).

PUBLISHERS' NOTE

THE series *History in the Making* is intended to illustrate from contemporary sources the thoughts and activities of working people engaged in historic movements for social and political freedom. Our history is inexhaustibly rich in material of this character: in autobiographies, memoirs and contemporary narratives, in trade union records, in the evidence given in courts of law and before Royal Commissions, and in the long succession of periodical literature inspired by movements of the people; but under present conditions all this wealth is becoming increasingly inaccessible to the general reader and to many students. Within the limited scope of small volumes we attempt to fill the gap, and it is hoped that the series may prove useful as a supplement to more general works. The broad guiding principle of selection is to exemplify theories, actions and organisations in their development from social conditions.

Wherever omissions have been made in the original text of an extract these are clearly indicated by the usual marks. Any inserted words are placed in square brackets.

The present volume is the first of three, illustrating the history of working-class movements in the nineteenth century. Volume II, edited by James Jefferys, covers the period 1848–80; Volume III, edited by Eric Hobsbawm, the period 1880–1900. Two volumes of seventeenth-century extracts, edited by Christopher Hill and Edmund Dell, are now in preparation, and the series will also include at least one twentieth-century volume.

INTRODUCTION

I

By 1815, when the twenty-one years of war against France ended, the industrial revolution had gone far towards transforming the face of Britain. The old, agrarian economy, with its domestic handicrafts, was giving way to a new industrial machine whose wheels were turned by steam. The process was accelerated by the compulsions of a large-scale war, which had penetrated deep into the heart of the nation's productive forces.

Land enclosure had increased the size of farms, and, with scientific improvements, raised agricultural productivity. The cotton-spinning industry was being organised more and more in steam driven mills. Iron smelting by coke had entirely replaced the old, charcoal process, and new methods of producing wrought iron were in general operation. Coal production was steadily mounting. A great building industry existed, second only to agriculture in the number of workers employed. The ancient craft of the potter had long since grown into a large-scale trade.

The whole trend of economic events was towards the elimination both of the independent artisan and the small workshop, and their replacement by a factory system using power machinery. But while the new was developing, the old lingered on. Much cotton weaving and most of the processes in the woollen and worsted industries were still carried on in small workshops or even in the home. The finished-metal trades were mainly organised in small scale units, and domestic "outwork" was general. Machinery had barely penetrated to flax, silk, or leather.

This, however, is evidence, not of an even and gradual transformation of the old into a new economy, but rather of the uneven development of industrialism in different sectors of production and in different parts of the country after the industrial revolution had begun. Once the first decisive inventions were put into operation the issue between the old and the new, with all its social implications, was never in doubt.

From 1815 to 1848 the tempo of change was very rapid. The enclosure of arable and "waste" land was almost completed, and machine methods were becoming common in the countryside. Steam power continued its conquest of cotton, and made decisive inroads into worsted and, more slowly, wool. The production of coal trebled and of iron quadrupled. Blast furnaces grew in size, efficiency and output. Engineering, though still organised in small workshops, made great forward strides and by 1847 "the mechanical engineer was getting ready to turn the world upside down." In all these developments the growth of rail transport played no small part. The railway was a revolutionary element speeding up industrialisation.

Thus by the middle of the century the first great steps in the establishment of a machine economy based on factory production had been taken, and the foundations laid for the vast expansion of the new system in the next twenty-five years. The existence of sectors where development was slow, where domestic "outwork" and small scale production continued, emphasise the positive character of the transformation which had occurred.

As the economic base of the social structure changed, new forces claimed political power. The oligarchy of the old ruling class, resulting from the victorious alliance of landowner and wealthy merchant in the seventeenth-century Revolution, was steadily losing ground. Whereas in 1815 it was still firmly entrenched, by 1848 the economic changes with the social struggles they generated had weakened it considerably; the Reform Act (1832) and the Repeal of the Corn Laws (1846) expressed the change. The growth of the factory system brought with it a class of industrial capitalists, the men who financed and organised the new productive forces. They were captains in an industrial army recruited from the landless labourers of the countryside, the domestic "outworkers" from the cottages, and the handicraftsmen of the towns, men, women and children, who were driven to the factories from the homesteads of England, Scotland, and especially Ireland. This was the new proletariat. By 1815 these two classes, masters and men, were achieving social cohesion.

The advances made in the thirty years after Waterloo enriched the industrial capitalists, clarified their common class interests and organised them more efficiently for political action. At the same time the growth of factory production drew the workers closer together, and fostered their class consciousness, a consciousness deepened by sufferings which were aggravated by the uneven and often localised development of the new system. Statistics which show improved real wage levels are of little value in the absence of information on short time working, unemployment, and the economic consequences of social displacement. They should not be allowed to obscure "the hardships, injustices and undeserved humiliations" which were heaped upon the workers. These are well documented in a great series of official reports which describe the long hours worked by young and old, the dangerous, unfenced machinery, the horrors of unregulated labour underground, and the filthy insanitary towns in which "the lower orders" were housed. Out of them emerges a clear picture of social insecurity and upheaval. The effect of the economic changes was cumulative, due to the process of displacement of handicraft by machinery, which involved degradation of status for different sections of workers at different times.

Such is the social background of the documents that follow. The workers themselves, whether in the mill or the mine, at the furnace or the handloom, at the bench or on the building job, did not feel that their conditions were improving, relatively or absolutely. To them, it is obvious from the contemporary press, industrial capitalism spelled poverty, insecurity, squalor, premature old age and death; and from these social conditions there arose a bitter class struggle which reached its greatest intensity in the years between 1815 and 1848. No sooner was peace made on the battlefield than the issue was joined on

B

the social field. It was a war involving shifting alliances between the classes; and if the forces of industrial Britain imposed new political disciplines on her ancient ruling caste, so deeply was it entrenched that often only the shadow of power was surrendered. The "oligarchy" was ready to stoop to retain at least part of its conquests.

The new middle classes, the mill-owners of Lancashire, the ironmasters of the Midlands, the shipbuilders of Thames and Tyne, vigorous, greedy, rich, were strong men in their localities. They were demanding a full share in the nation's councils, the right to be represented and to sit in Parliament. Deeply affected by the misgovernment of the Tories before 1832, by the recurrent financial crises, by the heavy burden and unfair incidence of taxation, they were concerned with the great problem of adjusting the old political to the new social balance, so that they, who understood the new capitalism, could mould the state in their own image. But just as their betters were ready to compromise, so were they, in order to gain entry into the charmed circle of rulers. For in spite of their differences, in solving which both classes attempted to win the workers as allies, their common interest, as opposed to the demands of the mass of the people, was paramount.

Toiling in the "dark Satanic mills" to create wealth which others enjoyed, the workers challenged both landlords and capitalists. It is this struggle of the working people for elementary human rights and the vision of a better future, which our documents are intended to illustrate. The main sources used are the working-class press, and the autobiographies and theoretical writings of the thinkers and leaders of the movement.

II

Extracts will be found from fourteen weekly newspapers, three of which, Cobbett's *Political Register* (1802–35), the *Poor Man's Guardian* (1831–5), and the *Northern Star* (1837–52), at times reached a wider public and wielded a more effective authority than any of their contemporaries. Those who conducted these papers never forgot that their main task was to educate and organise the people to win their social rights. Columns of the *Northern Star* are crowded with accounts of the movement; no meeting was too small to report, no incident too unimportant to record; a host of worker correspondents filled its pages with news that its respectable contemporaries would have scorned or been afraid to publish.

But the *Star* was able to build its enormous power only because it was heir to a great tradition. Starting publication at the height of the campaign against the new Poor Law in the industrial north, it carried on the struggle of the dispossessed with all the moral indignation and fervour infused into working-class journalism by Cobbett; its serious efforts in adult education continued along a pathway already traced by Carlile's *Republican*, Wooler's *Black Dwarf* and Hetherington's *Poor Man's Guardian*.

The great agitations had leaders, often self-educated men from the loom, the last, or the bench, who have left their personal records. There is Samuel Bamford, silk weaver and poet, whose descriptions of the movement in Lancashire deepen one's whole understanding of the forces that make history. There is sober William Lovett, the joiner, who loved to draw up programmes and addresses; his story is indispensable for the light it sheds on the mind of the skilled workers, of that educated minority accustomed to political manœuvre and negotiation, and able to hold its own in political argument with its masters. There is Joseph Arch, the agricultural labourer whose picture of the countryside ruled by squire and parson is unforgettable. Such stories and others, like those of Robert Owen, manufacturer and socialist, of George Jacob Holyoake, the metal worker, Thomas Cooper, the shoemaker, and Richard Pilling, the cotton-weaver, give a vivid picture of a period of economic change and social upheaval; in their pages is found none of the complacency of their contemporaries, the prolific middle-class apologists of capitalism.

The workers' movement produced a wealth of theoretical writing, political and economic. To-day, after a century of development away from the classical theories of political economy, the writings, for example, of Thomas Hodgskin, Francis Bray, William Thompson, and many others have been relegated to an undeserved obscurity. But these writers were true heirs of the great bourgeois economists of the classical period, whose doctrine they developed by giving to it a working-class content. Marx, who devoted great attention to Ricardo, also studied deeply his Radical successors and paid them many tributes both of praise and criticism. "The English factory workers," he wrote, "were the champions, not only of the English, but of the modern working class generally, as their theorists were the first to throw down the gauntlet to the theory of capital." These early Radical writers are part of the Socialist economic tradition. Like their classical predecessors they were *political* economists, with their feet firmly planted in the economic system of their day, a system which they tried to explain in order to change it for the better. Our few extracts from their work are enough to reveal these qualities. Hodgskin (No. 14), analysed the "fetish" of capital in order to defend the trade unions. Thompson (No. 15), disagreeing with Hodgskin's acceptance of "individual competition," offered as the only solution to economic inequality a form of Owenite socialism; whilst Bray (No. 48), attempted to analyse the "inequality" of exchanges under capitalism in order to win his readers for a fairer system.

In political theory the period saw a great advance towards an independent working class way of looking at the nature and development of social and political institutions, based largely on the economic analysis of writers like Hodgskin and Bray and on the philosophy of Owen. Bronterre O'Brien, above all, was feeling his way to a scientific analysis of the capitalist state, and to an understanding of the political, legal and cultural implications of capitalist property relations. Unlike Marx, however, he was not able to develop a coherent theory of the system.

In studying the change and development of the working class the student may find it useful to compare some of the documents relating to organisations, e.g. Nos. 16, 19, 20, 28, 33, 36, 37, 49, 50, 55, 63. For discussions on theory, including theories of trade unions, politics and socialism, he may find it suggestive to take together Nos. 14, 15*b*, 18, 20, 23, 32, 47, 48, 56.

III

Our material has been arranged first into a number of chronological phases.

1) *After Waterloo: Repression and Revolt* (1815–20), *pp.* 33–64

Cobbett's view of the war (No. 1) was commonly shared by the most thoughtful working people and was fully justified by the events of the post-war slump when the workers, especially in the north, raised the banner of reform. Cobbett was the prophet of the agitation. His *Address to the Journeymen and Labourers* had a profound effect; its demands, moderate as they may seem, were the advanced radical programme of the time. The movement, in fact, was carrying on from the point where wartime repression had interrupted its development: from the struggles of the 1790's, the days of Tom Paine and of the Corresponding Societies. Among its heroes was still the venerable Major Cartwright, and its present leaders, Cobbett, Henry Hunt, and Richard Carlile among others, stood for programmes demanding a reform of parliament, the cleansing of corruption, reduction of taxation and the national debt, and freedom of speech and thought. The bastions of the oligarchy had first to be stormed before the workers could develop an independent policy. In this situation the moderate demands of the radicals had a revolutionary significance and rallied the support of the people. At the same time the middle classes, who would have benefited from the radical programme, were as a whole hostile to the workers' movement from fear of the forces it might generate.

These forces, on which Bamford sheds brilliant light, were gathering strength. The Government set out to suppress them. The Habeas Corpus Act was suspended (No. 5) and the movement driven underground. Suppression bred violent reaction. The Six Gag Acts (No. 9) were followed by the actions of the Scottish rebels (No. 11) and the Cato Street Conspiracy (No. 10). It is easy to denounce Arthur Thistlewood, the conspirator, as a crazy fanatic, a kind of Guy Fawkes of reform. But Cobbett was no terrorist and his reaction to Cato Street was the full publication of Thistlewood's defence and an injunction to his son to disseminate it in the United States. Such individual terrorist actions were the natural outcome of a regime stained with the memory of Peterloo (No. 8) and disgraced by its use of agents provocateurs (No. 6).

While, however, the objectives of the Parliamentary reformers of 1815–1820 were limited, the consolidation of industrialism was giving rise to more radical policies. Robert Owen now became a portent in the working class movement. Previously known as a benevolent factory reformer with advanced ideas of industrial organisation and unorthodox views on human nature, whose main appeal was addressed to the upper class, he now began to put forward the socialist conceptions which were to have such an enduring influence on the next generation of working-class leaders (No. 7).

2) *Trade Union Theory and Action* (1824–38), *pp.* 65–107

The Combination Laws of 1799–1800, aimed at destroying trade unionism, had not succeeded in their object, though, supplemented by the common law and ancient statutes, they were ruthlessly used to keep down wages. It is often said that there was little or no direct workers' agitation for repeal of the laws and the Webbs point out that the more enlightened workers' leaders were concerned more with thorough parliamentary reform. A more adequate summary of the situation might be that under the repressive Tory regime a reform of the system of government seemed the only way of securing any elementary rights to the workers, so clearly were measures like those prohibiting trade unionism examples of class legislation. The struggle against such laws was, however, carried on in the most practical way, namely by refusal to observe them—another form of the direct action which took more violent paths in other cases.

The strong persistence of trade unionism impressed the masters, and the Select Committee on Artisans and Machinery (No. 12) was set up at a time when the trade revival of the early 1820's had made the government less afraid of working class organisation; leading ministers were also being influenced by economic theories "proving" that unions could not in any case influence wages, which were regulated by "economic laws." The evidence of the Committee showed not only the application of the Combination Laws to the workers only, but their ineffectiveness. Repeal was carried through. Francis Place, who had been mainly responsible for engineering the Committee, had sanguinely hoped that repeal would remove the sense of grievance which he thought lay behind all these dangerous illegal union activities, and that the unions would now fade out and leave wages to find their "natural" level. He was fated to disappointment. Repeal was followed by intenser activity, and the government, pressed by sections of the employers, took measures against it (No. 13).

But the unions continued, and later, in the crisis of 1830, a mighty workers' movement developed, both in the industrial and political fields. Trade unionism grew into trades unionism. Beginning in Lancashire with the National Association for the Protection of Labour (No. 16), the movement, due to the stress of economic change and to the exploitation by the middle classes of the parliamentary reform agitation for their own advantage, reached a high level of class consciousness in the Grand

National Consolidated Trade Union of 1834 (Nos. 20–4). What stands out in the policies of the G.N.C.T.U. is a vision of the future, when labour will "walk with its head erect," of a community of producers, organising their lives on co-operative principles and thus recreating humanity. The attempt to unite the trade unions with the control of production was a social revolutionary attempt. The emphasis on constructive social and economic programmes based on the unions, and the opposition to "politics" was largely due to Owen, who identified politics with the dreary parliamentary manoeuvring which had brought such disappointment to his early plans. At the same time the General Strike plan of William Benbow (No. 17) brilliantly expressed the revolutionary mood of the unionists, whose militant industrial action the Utopian Owen did not approve.

The failure of the G.N.C.T.U. was due to weak organisation and insufficient political clarity, as well as to the repressive action of government and employers. But the spirit evinced in George Loveless's account of Tolpuddle and the solidarity described in the London demonstration of sympathy for the "martyrs" (No. 22) could not easily be extinguished; the strike and trial of the Glasgow cotton spinners in 1837 (No. 24) showed its persistence in face of the continued antagonism of the authorities.

3) *The Village* (1815–42), *pp.* 109–19

Although Britain was now an industrial country, the largest single group of the population was still occupied in agriculture. The labourers, after the social changes in the countryside, were a great force numerically, and were smarting under the hardships of the new society. The movement of 1830–1 in the villages (No. 26) should be seen as part of the general unrest that was sweeping the country in those years of crisis, prior to the Reform Act, and of which Tolpuddle was another expression. The spirit of independence shown by the family of Joseph Arch (No. 27) was more general than is often imagined.

Chartism was later to take firm hold in many villages and country towns.

4) *The Struggle For Social and Political Rights* (1830–40), *pp.* 121–66

In the economic crisis of the 1830's the parliamentary reform movement had reawakened. On the one hand, the pressure of the industrial and commercial middle classes, organised through Political Unions for the extension of the franchise, was telling on a section of the oligarchy. On the other hand, the workers' demands were now clearer and their political understanding higher than before. New men had risen to share the leadership with Hunt and Cobbett, the men of the National Union of the Working Classes (No. 28), William Lovett and Henry Hetherington, and the editor of the *Poor Man's Guardian*, Bronterre O'Brien. They drew the correct political conclusions from the campaign for the 1832 Reform Act which enfranchised "the moneymongers and shopocrats" and gave the workers nothing. They had bitter experience of the way the mass pressure of the people had been used to frighten the Tory landlords and win a middle class victory.

Thus when the revolutionary trade union wave subsided and a temporary economic recovery was again followed by crisis, Chartism developed in full strength as an independent workers' movement. Sections of the middle classes supported it, but this support was now given on working class terms to a working class programme. The pace was set, the agitation led and organised, by working men's associations. The middle class element was faltering and hesitant and fell away during the first crisis of the movement. The Chartists stood on their own feet determined not to be used as a cat's-paw for the ends of others.

The Charter had been drawn up by the skilled or independent artisans of the London Workingmen's Association (No. 33) in conjunction with a few middle-class

M.Ps., but its main support came from the factory
workers, the handicraftsmen threatened with displacement and the unemployed of the north. All were united
for the Six Points, but their differences as to tactics were
reflected in the leadership. Feargus O'Connor, owner of
the *Northern Star*, appealed powerfully to the "fustian
jackets and unshorn chins"; Lovett represented those
skilled men whose work was relatively unaffected by the
new factory system.

Chartism was more than a movement for parliamentary
reform. The masses who were its core fought for social
aims. Confused and diverse though these were, they
flowed naturally from the poverty and degradation which
since 1815 seemed to be the permanent lot of the worker.
It was this sense of humiliation which gave the emotional
fire to the agitation against the 1834 Poor Law (No. 34).
Its provisions were regarded with hatred and contempt by
its intended victims, and they began that great series of
demonstrations which, for many years, threw the North
of England into a turmoil. In reading the *Northern Star*
for 1838 we get the impression of a mass movement at
white heat, determined in purpose and revolutionary in
tone. The violence of the anti-Poor Law speeches merged
naturally into "physical force" Chartism, and into
that debate, so vital at the time, as to whether the
Chartists would be justified in using force to meet force
(No. 42).

This debate was central to the deliberations of the first
Chartist Convention which met in February, 1839
(No. 40). When it dispersed in September there followed
the abortive rising at Newport (No. 46). There is little
doubt that there was some plan of action that went
beyond South Wales. But what we know of the revolt
illustrates the gap between intention and organisation,
the divisions among the leaders, that underlay the general
failure of the Chartists to win their demands. The movement now met the full force of government repression, but
that it was not quenched the next years showed un-
mistakably.

5) *Industrial and Political Action* (1840–8), *pp.* 167–207

When the first shock of defeat had passed, Chartism, with most of its active spirits in prison, began to regroup its forces. One battle was lost but the struggle could not be given up. The problem of organisation (based on local area groups, "classes") was successfully tackled (No. 49). Propaganda was renewed. New dangers had to be faced. There was the middle class bid to win workers' support for the anti-Corn Law League, and their attempt through the Complete Suffrage movement to capture the leadership of the campaign for parliamentary reform. What is significant is the tenacity with which the Chartist leaders held on to their cause, scarcely to be deflected by other slogans whose class origins were suspect, even though they had mass appeal.

During the economic crisis of 1842 intensive agitation developed. The Petition of that year (No. 50) shows a keener class understanding, born of the first struggles, and reveals the distance travelled since the first Chartist Petition of 1839 (No. 37). The climax was reached in the General Strike of August, in which the contention of middle class and working class interests is clearly illuminated. The strike was accompanied by widespread concerted and sometimes violent action, for which the Chartist leaders were unprepared. Once more the law intervened with force and the movement was suppressed.

After 1842, Chartism, guided by Feargus O'Connor in his later phase, took a different turning. Activity continued and was directed more to the trade unions. But the organisation was increasingly absorbed by the "Land Plan" to settle workers as small holders (No. 55). This was partly a reaction to the years of agitation, which, not followed up by "Ulterior Measures," had failed to win the Charter. The plan was essentially defeatist since it looked back to the pre-industrial economy instead of strengthening the struggle against capitalism, but it attempted a constructive response to the "cheap bread" slogan of the anti-Corn Law League which was meeting with increasing support from the people, as the debates in the Convention of 1845 showed. The improving economic situation had undoubtedly set new problems to the movement. Capitalism, in spite of recurring crises, was on the threshold of an era of great expansion and the middle classes, conscious of their growing wealth and strength, were more united than ever in their anti-Chartist front. The repeal of the Corn Laws in 1846, hastened by the potato famine of 1845, added to their strength.

The new situation was reflected in the policies of the trade unions. Union influence was growing, as the columns of the *Northern Star* amply show. But the programme of the National Association of United Trades of 1845 (No. 63) must be contrasted with that of the unions of 1834 (Nos. 20, 21, 23). The emphasis now was on the immediate problem of improving the workers' position "at the point of production" rather than on visionary ideas of a golden socialist or co-operative future. That there was no weakening however in the spirit of struggle, the story of the miners' strike of 1844 showed. What the new unions had gained was a keener understanding of the strength of capitalism and consequently of the need for new forms of effort.

The great crisis of 1847 revived mass agitation. Many Chartist candidates stood in the election of that year, when O'Connor was returned as member for Nottingham (No. 58). True, he was speaking a different language from that of ten years earlier; but the victory was no less a Chartist one.

With the French Revolution of 1848 feeling rose yet higher; a new convention was summoned, a new petition prepared. But once more the movement stumbled over the old obstacle—insufficient organisation, diversity of aims and no united leadership. Much has been made by historians of the "fiasco" of the third Chartist petition, of inflated claims and false signatures, and not enough of the defence put up by O'Connor, or the time-honoured Home Office system of sabotaging the workers' movement from within. The Government, with all its apparent contempt for the Chartists, was careful enough in its preparations for their suppression.

1848 was the end of an epoch. The new economic and social conditions, which had already made their mark, were to create new forms of struggle. But the traditions of the thirties and forties were never forgotten. The sons and grandsons of the Chartists could look back with pride on the first independent movement of the workers.

IV

Our last three sections are devoted to certain lines of development which can be traced throughout the whole period.

6) *Producers and Consumers, pp.* 209–22

The success in winning *shorter working hours* has usually been ascribed to the efforts of philanthropists like Sadler and Shaftesbury. Such men did much to stir the upper class conscience on the horrors suffered by the factory children and to carry through reforms. But that there was a persistent movement, closely linked to the factories and organised in the Short Time Committees, is all too often forgotten. "The Ten Hours Bill," said Feargus O'Connor, "is one of the legs of Chartism." Both unionists and Chartists well knew the importance of the demand for shorter hours and for the protection of women and children from the evils of unregulated capitalism.

From its earliest days *co-operation* was part of the wider workers' movement, and was organised under the same leadership. Robert Owen, in spite of his original antagonism to trading societies, became the channel through which co-operative ideas filtered through to the people. These ideas took firm root among them. But it was not until the plan of the Rochdale Pioneers was applied that a suitable form was found within which co-operation could flourish in a capitalist environment.

7) *The Struggle for Freedom of Speech and Thought, pp.* 223–39

This page of British history is often misunderstood. It was the working class movement that led the fight to win freedom of speech and thought, thus proving itself the heir of a great tradition and carrying on the struggle waged by Milton and the puritans in the great revolution of the seventeenth century. The social situation had changed. The descendants of those middle class revolutionaries were now resisting free speech, which had become the weapon of a new class struggling against oppression. The puritans had demanded freedom of religion, but Carlile, Hetherington and Holyoake, renewing the traditions of Tom Paine and reinforced by Owen, fought against religion itself, as a fetter on social progress. In Hetherington pre-eminently the fight for rationalism and for a free press are seen together (Nos. 69–73). He and his fellows, with anti-clericals like Cobbett, made a working class press and sane discussion of the church and religion possible. Their fight had begun before 1815, and in 1848 it was not over. But in these years the capital effort was made that ensured future success.

8) *Internationalism, pp.* 241–54

Internationalism, an integral feature of the Labour Movement to-day, has deep roots in our history. Bronterre O'Brien thought it a public duty to write a vindication of Robespierre, and to translate Buonarotti's *Conspiracy for Equality* in order to popularise the work of Baboeuf and the early French communists. Cobbett wrote of the "glorious event at Paris" when the Bourbons were dethroned in 1830. The *Northern Star* gave ample publicity to international societies such as the Fraternal Democrats (No. 79), with which Marx and Engels were in association. The whole working class press was deeply concerned at the oppression of the Irish people. Trade unionists and Chartists alike constantly criticised the foreign policies of both Whigs and Tories; it was no accident that Harney, the Chartist expert on foreign affairs, stood against the Foreign Secretary, Palmerston, in the General Election of 1847. And it was just as natural that the organised movement expressed its solidarity with the French revolutionists of 1848 with much the same feelings as the earlier radicals had greeted the events of 1789. Actions such as these strengthened the traditions of internationalism which took new forms in the period that followed.

Note on Sources

Unfortunately, the printed sources of much material quoted here are now to be found in few libraries apart from the British Museum, and are otherwise not easily available. Exceptions are the writings of Cobbett and Owen, which explains their brief treatment in the present selection. In two cases (Nos. 19b)c) and 38b) where wartime damage has rendered the originals inaccessible, quotation has been made from a secondary source. Of the works used, some original editions or modern reprints that may be found in public libraries or are otherwise reasonably accessible are listed below:

Everyman Library (Dent): *A New View of Society*, by Robert Owen. Bohn's Library (Bell): *Autobiography*, by Robert Owen; *The Life and Struggles of William Lovett*; *Pioneers of Land Reform* (by Thomas Spence and others). Cobbett Press: *The Opinions of William Cobbett* (a selection from the *Political Register*), edited by G. D. H. and M. Cole. (There are various reprints of Cobbett's other works, including, in the Everyman Library, *Rural Rides*.) London School of Economics: *Labour's Wrongs and Labour's Remedy*, by Francis Bray. Labour Publishing Co: *Labour Defended* by Thomas Hodgskin (edited by G. D. H. Cole (1922)). Allen and Unwin: *The Condition of the Working Class in England in 1844*, by Frederick Engels. Hutchinson: *The Story of His Life*, by Joseph Arch. Fisher Unwin (Benn): *Sixty Years of an Agitator's Life*, by G. J. Holyoake. Summerbell (Newcastle): *The Miners of Northumberland and Durham*, by R. Fynes.

For further study the reader should consult the bibliographies given in *The Common People*, by G. D. H. Cole and R. W. Postgate (Methuen), and in *English Radicalism, 1832–1852*, by S. Maccoby (Allen and Unwin).

Acknowledgments

I wish to make the following acknowledgments. Dona Torr has always been ready with encouragement, advice, and practical help. I owe a great deal to Mr. H. L. Beales for his direction of my Chartist studies from their inception. My thanks are due to Mr. James Jefferys for some valuable suggestions, to Mrs. E. Propper for indispensable technical assistance, to Mrs. W. E. Trotman for help in transcription always generously given, to Mr M. Jenkins for his kind efforts to trace some documents in Manchester, and above all to my wife for the many hours she devoted to the manuscript.

MAX MORRIS.

Part One

AFTER WATERLOO: REPRESSION AND REVOLT, 1815–20

1. PEACE, 1815

From *Cobbett's Weekly Political Register*, September 25th, 1815.
On the war, see also Nos. 9, 74.

THE war, which began in 1793, is now over. The troops are not all come home, the ships are not all paid off, the account is not wound up; but the war is over. Social Order is restored; the French are again in the power of the Bourbons; the Revolution is at an end; no change has been effected in England; our Boroughs, and our Church, and Nobility and all have been preserved; our government tells us, that we have covered ourselves with glory. . . .

2. COBBETT'S ADDRESS TO THE JOURNEYMEN AND LABOURERS, 1816

The effect of this Address on the minds of the workers was, says Cobbett, "prodigious." Over 200,000 copies were sold within the month. It heralded the beginning of new mass movements, directed towards Parliamentary Reform. Cobbett now issued a twopenny edition of his shilling *Register* (*Twopenny Trash*) avoiding the newspaper tax by omitting news items. He soon advanced from the demand for taxpayers' suffrage (below) to that of "universal" (adult male) suffrage. The extract is from *Cobbett's Weekly Political Register*, November 2nd, 1816.

. . . THE real strength, and all the resources of the country ever have sprung . . . from the *labour* of its people. . . . With the correct idea of your own worth in your minds, with what indignation must you hear yourselves called the Populace, the Rabble, the Mob, the Swinish Multitude. . . .

The times in which we live are full of peril. . . . As to the *cause* of our present miseries, it is the *enormous amount of the taxes* which the government compels us to pay for the support of its army, its placemen, its pensioners etc. and for the payment of the interest of its debt . . . the tax gatherers do not, indeed, come to *you* and demand money of you: but, there are few articles which you use, in the purchase of which you do not pay a tax. . . .

The weight of the Poor rate, which must increase while the present system continues, alarms the Corrupt, who plainly see, that what is paid to relieve you *they* cannot have. Some of them therefore hint at your *early* marriages as a great evil, and a Clergyman named Malthus, has seriously proposed measures for checking you in this respect . . . while labourers and journeymen . . . are actually paying taxes for the support of these lords' and ladies' children, these cruel and insolent men propose that they shall have no relief and that their children ought to be *checked*. . . .

The remedy . . . consists wholely and solely of such a *reform* in the Commons' or People's House of Parliament, as shall give to every payer of *direct taxes* a vote at elections, and as shall cause the members to be *elected annually*. . . .

. . . You should neglect no opportunity of doing all that is within your power to give support to the cause of Reform. *Petition* is the channel of your sentiments . . . you ought to attend at every public meeting within your reach. You ought to read to, and assist each other in coming at a competent knowledge of all public matters. . . . I exhort you to proceed in a peaceable and lawful manner, but at the same time, to proceed with zeal and resolution in the attainment of this object. . . .

3. THE LAND: SOCIETY OF SPENCEAN PHILANTHROPISTS, 1812–20

While Cobbett gave the lead for a Parliamentary reform agitation, other working-class reformers pursued older aims. The small Society of Spencean Philanthropists (1812–20) was named after Thomas Spence (1750–1814) whose teaching had carried on the long tradition of revolt against private appropriation of the land; he demanded its transfer to parishes and municipalities with rent as the single tax. In December, 1816, the Spenceans organised a meeting in Spa Fields, London, from which a riot developed. The Government made this an excuse for setting up Secret Committees to "inquire" into radical activities. The Committees' reports, based mainly on the evidence of spies and provocateurs, led to the suspension of the Habeas Corpus Act in March, 1817 (No. 5). The prosecution of the Spencean leaders for high treason had to be dropped after one was acquitted by the jury.

The Spencean programme originated from Spence's famous lecture of 1775, quoted below from *Pioneers of Land Reform*, Bell, 1920, pp. 5–9.

. . . THAT property in land and liberty among men in a state of nature ought to be equal, few, one would be fain to hope, would be foolish enough to deny. Therefore, taking this to be granted, the country of any people, in a native state, is properly their common, in which each of them has an equal property, with free liberty to sustain himself and family with the animals, fruits and other products thereof. Thus such a people reap jointly the whole advantages of their country, or neighbourhood, without having their right in so doing called in question by any, not even by the most selfish and corrupt. . . .

Hence it is plain that the land or earth, in any country or neighbourhood, with everything in or on the same, or pertaining thereto, belongs at all times to the living inhabitants of the said country or neighbourhood in an equal manner. . . .

If we look back to the origin of the present nations, we shall see that the land, with all its appurtenances, was claimed by a few, and divided among themselves, in as assured a manner as if they had manufactured it and it had been the work of their own hands; and by being unquestioned, or not called to an account for such usurpations and unjust claims, they fell into a habit of thinking, or, which is the same thing to the rest of mankind, of acting as if the earth was made for or by them, and did not scruple to call it their own property. . . .

. . . Thus men may not live in any part of this world, not even where they are born, but as strangers, and by the permission of the pretender to the property thereof; which permission is, for the most part, paid extravagantly for. . . .

4. THE MARCH OF THE BLANKETEERS, 1817

This "hunger march," largely of weavers, started for London from Manchester on March 10th, 1817, to petition the Prince Regent. The extracts are from *a*) *Passages in the Life of a Radical*, by Samuel Bamford, 1844, pp. 32–4, and *b*) *The Black Dwarf*, September 10th, 1817. Bamford, who disapproved of the expedition, was a domestic silk weaver of Middleton, Lancs, and a leading Radical of the period. *The Black Dwarf* was edited by Jonathan Wooler, one of the pioneers of Radical journalism, who expressed the popular indignation at the imprisonment without trial of eight Blanketeers.

a) THE meeting took place according to appointment; but I not being there, my brief description must be taken as the account of others. The assemblage consisted almost entirely of operatives, four or five thousands in number; and was held on that piece of ground (Saint Peter's Field) which afterwards obtained so melancholy a celebrity. Many of the individuals were observed to have blankets, rugs, or large coats, rolled up and tied, knap-sack like, on their backs; some carried bundles under their arms; some had papers, supposed to be petitions rolled up; some had stout walking sticks. The magistrates came upon the field and read the riot act, and the meeting was afterwards dispersed by the military, and special constables; and twenty-nine persons were apprehended. . . . On the riot act being read, about three hundred persons left the meeting to commence their march to London. Some of them formed a straggling line in Mosley-street, and marched along Piccadilly, being continually joined by others, until the whole body was collected, near Ardwick Green. . . .

. . . A body of yeomanry soon afterwards followed those simple-minded men, and took possession of the bridge at Stockport. Many then turned back to their homes; a body of them crossed the river below, and entered Cheshire; several received sabre wounds, and one man was shot dead on Lancashire hill. Of those who persisted in their march it is only necessary to say, that they arrived at nine o'clock at night in the market place at Macclesfield, being about one hundred and eighty in number. Some of them lay out all night, and took the earliest dawn to find their way home. Some were well lodged and hospitably entertained by friends; some paid for quarters, and some were quartered in prison. Few were those who marched the following morning. About a score arrived at Leek, and six only were known to pass Ashbourne bridge. And so ended the blanket expedition!

b) The poor men at Manchester, who were represented as designing to wrap both Houses of Parliament, and the barracks at Knightsbridge, in their blankets, and throw them into the Thames, have all been acquitted. . . . Did I say acquitted? why, *they have not even been tried.* The ministers dared to accuse them of treason and riot when the agents of those ministers made all the riot that existed: —and the treason was committed *against* and *not by these blanket men.* They were guilty of exercising the right of petitioning, when the soldiers surrounded them and picked from the numbers whom they pleased. . . . The men thus *illegally* seized were imprisoned for months;— they courted a trial to demonstrate the tyrannical manner in which they had been treated: some bravely refused to give bail . . . others were requested to plead guilty and they would be discharged. . . . This was also nobly resisted. The day of the trial arrives and the PROSECUTOR DARE NOT PROCEED; but makes a parade of his beneficence in not proceeding against men, whom he had before punished by a long imprisonment. . . . By all the rules of justice, these men possess a right of redress from those who have imprisoned them upon a false accusation and punished them without a crime. . . .

5. SUSPENSION OF THE HABEAS CORPUS ACT, 1817

From Bamford, *op. cit.*, Chapter VII. Besides Cobbett, several Radical leaders are mentioned. "Orator" Henry Hunt, famous popular agitator, was main speaker at "Peterloo" (No. 8), after which he was gaoled; later M.P. for Preston (1830). Sir Francis Burdett and Lord Cochrane, popular aristocratic Radicals of the early period, sat together for Westminster, 1807–18. "The worthy old Major," Major John Cartwright (1740–1824), whose steadfast propaganda for manhood suffrage began with his pamphlet, *Take Your Choice* (1776), promoted after 1815 the Hampden Clubs for constitutional reform to which artisans like Bamford belonged. Cartwright barely escaped imprisonment for treason when nearly eighty years old.

Suspension of Habeas Corpus legalised imprisonment without trial. Added to this were various new repressive laws.

PERSONAL liberty not being now secure from one hour to another, many of the leading reformers were induced to quit their homes, and seek concealment where they could obtain it. Those who could muster a few pounds, or who had friends to give them a frugal welcome, or had trades with which they could travel, disappeared like swallows at the close of summer, no one knew whither. The single men stayed away altogether; the married ones would occasionally steal back at night to their wan-cheeked families, perhaps to divide with them some trifle they had saved during their absence—perhaps to obtain a change of linen or other garment for future conceal-ment—but most of all, as would naturally be the case, to console, and be consoled by their wives and little ones. Perhaps one had found an asylum amongst kind friends, and had brought home a little hoard, the fruits of his own industry and carefulness, or of their generosity. Perhaps he had been wandering in want, not daring to make himself known, until his beard disguised him, his shoes and stockings were trampled from his feet, and his linen was in rags; when at length, worn out and reckless, he would venture home, like the wearied bird which found no place to rest. Perhaps he had been discovered to be a reform leader, and had been threatened, mayhap pursued, and like a hunted hare now returned to the place of former repose. Then he would come home stealthily under cover of darkness; his wife would rush into his arms, his little ones would be about his knees, looking silent pleasure—for they, poor things, like nestling birds, had learned to be mute in danger.

But with all precautions, it did sometimes happen, that in such moments of mournful joy the father would be seized, chained, and torn from his family before he had time to bless them or to receive their blessings and tears. Such scenes were of frequent occurrence, and have thrown a melancholy retrospection over those days. Private revenge or political differences were gratified by secret and often false information handed to the police. The country was distracted by rumours of treasonable discoveries, and apprehensions of the traitors, whose fate was generally predicted to be death or perpetual imprisonment . . . and it was frequently intimated to me, through some very kind relations in law, that I and some of my acquaintance would soon be arrested. . . . The cloud of gloom and mistrust hung over the whole country.

The suspension of the Habeas Corpus Act was a measure the result of which we young reformers could not judge, save by report, and that was of a nature to cause anxiety in the most indifferent of us. The proscriptions, imprisonments, trials, and banishments of 1792, were brought to our recollections by the similarity of our situation to those of the sufferers of that period. It seemed as if the sun of freedom were gone down, and a rayless expanse of oppression had finally closed over us.

Cobbett, in terror of imprisonment, had fled to America; Sir Francis Burdett had enough to do in keeping his own arms free; Lord Cochrane was threatened, but quailed not; Hunt was still somewhat turbulent, but he was powerless—for he had lost the genius of his influence when he lost Cobbett, and was now almost like Sampson shorn and blind. The worthy old Major remained at his post, brave as a lion—serene as an unconscious child; and also, in the rush and tumult of that time, almost as little noticed. . . . To complete our misfortunes, our chapel-keeper, in the very tremor of fear, turned the key upon us and declared we should no longer meet in the place.

Our Society, thus houseless, became divided and dismayed; hundreds slunk home to their looms, nor dared to come out, save like owls at nightfall, when they would perhaps steal through bye-paths or behind hedges, or down some clough, to hear the news at the next cottage. Some might be seen chatting with and making themselves agreeable to our declared enemies; but these were few, and always of the worst character. Open meetings thus being suspended, secret ones ensued; they were originated at Manchester, and assembled under various pretexts. Sometimes they were termed "benefit societies"; sometimes "botanical meetings"; "meetings for the relief of the families of imprisoned reformers," or "of those who had fled the country"; but their real purpose, divulged only to the initiated, was to carry into effect the night attack on Manchester, the attempt at which had before failed for want of arrangement and co-operation.

6. A HOME OFFICE SPY

Throughout 1817 the Home Office was particularly active
in using *agents provocateurs* to incite workers to acts of violence
in order that excuse could be shown for punitive action
against the whole reform movement. Cleary was associated
with the most notorious of all the spies, Oliver, in a plot
which resulted in the execution of four Derbyshire "rebels"
and the transportation and imprisonment of many others.
Henry Hunt exposed the whole affair in *The Green Bag Plot*,
1819, pp. 13–15, from which the following extract is taken.
See also No. 10.

. . . FROM what I saw of *Mr. Cleary* at that time I was
determined to watch his proceedings very narrowly, and
at all events to have nothing more to do with any political
meetings where he was concerned. . . . When I went to
Manchester I made enquiry amongst the delegates who
had been in London . . . and it was with no small surprise
I learnt that EVERY MAN who had attended these meetings
had warrants issued against them by the Secretary of
State, the moment the Habeas Corpus Act was suspended,
except the said *Mr. Cleary*. I found that these Delegates,
seven in number, had attended at the Cock in Grafton
Street *by the appointment of Mr. Cleary*. That when they got
there *Mr. Cleary* led the conversation, and in the words
of Mr. Mitchell... "After repeated attempts to check what
we thought great indiscretion in Mr. Cleary, who did not
know any of us even by NAME at the time, except myself,
for he confined his conversation to topics of a revolutionary or insurrectionary tendency, he said, 'It was madness or folly for the leaders among the people to think of
anything but physical force.' I more than once attempted
to turn the conversation, which I thought very indiscreet,
yet I did not succeed, for he stuck more closely to those
subjects, than ever Oliver did in conversation with me.
At length Mr. Cleary proposed EXCHANGING ADDRESSES,
which was done, as he stated, that he might correspond or

SEND DOWN into the Country COMMUNICATIONS OF IMPORT-ANCE. Of course we could have no suspicion at that time of Mr. Cleary, having found him, with Major Cartwright, the secretary of the Hampden Club, etc., etc., which gave currency to his acts, and stamped patriotism, as we thought, on almost every word that came from him. . . ."

The enigma is unravelled . . . how is it that this fellow has been enabled to live like a gentleman . . . for the last six or seven years, without any visible means of gaining an honest livelihood. . . . I have performed a public duty in exposing the extent of *espionage* and the *employment of Spies* by this inquisitorial government. . . .

7. ROBERT OWEN'S PLAN FOR SOCIETY

This imaginary dialogue was written by Owen (July, 1817) in amplification of the "Plan" first briefly outlined in 1816 and presented in his Report to the Committee of the Association for the Relief of the Manufacturing and Labouring Poor, 1817. First conceived as a plan to relieve unemployment, the scheme grew into one for a reorganisation of the whole of society. From *The Life of Robert Owen, written by Himself*, 1857, Vol. I A Appendix I (2).

Q. . . . To what causes do you attribute the distress existing among the poor and working classes?

A. To a misapplication of the existing powers of production in the country . . . when compared to the wants and demands for those productions. Much of our natural power, consisting of the physical and intellectual faculties of human beings, is now . . . unproductive . . . while a very large part of our artificial or mechanical agency is employed to produce that which is of little real value to society. . . .

Q. Does your experience enable you to suggest a more advantageous application of these productive powers?

A. . . . They may, with ease, be so directed as to remove speedily the present distress of the labouring poor and . . . carry the prosperity of the country to a point much higher than it has ever yet attained.

Q. How can this be done?

A. By forming well-digested arrangements to occupy the apparent surplus of the labouring poor, who are competent to work, in productive employment, in order that they may maintain themselves first, and afterwards contribute to bear their proportion of the expenses of the state.

Q. Do the means exist by which employment could be given to the unoccupied of the working classes?

A. . . . The country possesses the most ample means to attain this object . . . land unemployed; land imperfectly cultivated; money employed unprofitably; manual powers of labour idle . . . artificial or mechanical agency almost unlimited. . . .

Q. How can they be put into action?

A. By bringing them all into useful and profitable combinations, so as to create limited communities of individuals, on the principle of united labour and expenditure, having their basis in agriculture and in which all should have mutual and common interests.

Q. What are your reasons for recommending such a combination of human powers?

A. . . . the very superior advantages which each person could derive by this means beyond any application of his own exertions for his own exclusive purposes. . . . Communities of 500 to 1,500 persons, founded on the principles of united labour and expenditure, and having their basis in agriculture, might be arranged so as to give the following advantages to the labouring poor, and through them to all the other classes. . . . All the labour . . . would be . . . directed first to procure . . . abundance of all that was necessary for their comfortable existence; next, they would obtain the means to enable them to unlearn many . . . of the bad habits which the present defective arrangements of society have forced upon them: then, to give only the best habits and dispositions to the rising generation, and thus withdraw those circumstances from society which separate man from man, and introduce others, whose entire tendency shall be to unite them in one general interest. . . . They will afterwards be enabled to cultivate the far more valuable, the intellectual part of their natures; that part which, when properly directed, will discover how much may yet be put into practice to promote human happiness. . . .

. . . It is found that when men work together for a common interest, each performs his part more advantageously for himself and for society, than when employed for others. . . .

Q. But will not the parties dispute perpetually about the division and possession of the property?

A. Certainly not . . . now . . . the mass of mankind

cannot procure sufficient to support themselves in ordinary comfort without great exertion and anxiety; they therefore acquire, under the influence of a strong necessity, a tenacious love of that property which costs them so much to procure; thus making the feeling itself appear . . . as one implanted by nature in the constitution. No conclusion can, however, be more erroneous. . . .

Q. Is it not to be feared that such arrangements would produce a dull uniformity of character, repress genius? . . .

A. It appears to me that quite the reverse of all this will follow; that the means provided in these establishments will give every stimulus to bring forth and to perfect the best parts only of every character, by furnishing the inhabitants with such valuable instruction . . . and by affording sufficient leisure and freedom from anxiety to promote the natural direction of their powers. . . . As for the probability of a dull uniformity of character being produced. . . . From the hour they are born, treated with uniform kindness, directed by reason, . . . the physical powers trained and cultivated . . . the mental faculties furnished with adequate data . . . children so trained, men so circumstanced would soon become, not a dull uniform race but beings full of health, activity, and energy. . . . So far from genius being depressed, it will receive every aid to enable it to exert itself, with unrestrained delight, and with the highest benefit to mankind. . . .

D

8. PETERLOO, 16 AUGUST, 1819

The demonstration at St. Peter's Fields, Manchester, immortalised as the Massacre of Peterloo, was the climax of the movement for parliamentary reform in the North. Eleven were killed, and over 400 wounded—many of them women—by the military without the slightest provocation by the crowd.

Extracts *a*), *b*), *c*) are from Bamford, *op. cit.*, Chapters 30, 33, 35, 36; *d*) is from the Place Papers, Add. MSS. 27,837 (179). Francis Place (1771–1854), master tailor, was a leading Radical whose shop at Charing Cross was a political centre. Working in the background, he later helped to promote the repeal of the Combination Acts (Nos. 12–13). Historians of the working class are deeply indebted to his careful collections of contemporary documents, now in the British Museum.

John Cam Hobhouse, Lord Broughton, Byron's close friend and executor, was later a Whig Minister. See No. 77.

a) PREPARATIONS

IT was deemed expedient that this meeting should be as morally effective as possible, and, that it should exhibit a spectacle such as had never before been witnessed in England. We had frequently been taunted by the Press, with our ragged, dirty appearance, at these assemblages; with the confusion of our proceedings, and the mob-like crowds in which our numbers were mustered; and we determined that, for once at least, these reflections should not be deserved,—that we would disarm the bitterness of our political opponents by a display of cleanliness, sobriety, and decorum, such as we never before had exhibited. In short, we would deserve their respect by shewing that we respected ourselves, and knew how to exercise our rights of meeting, as it were well Englishmen always should do,—in a spirit of sober thoughtfulness; respectful, at the same time, to the opinions of others.

"CLEANLINESS," "SOBRIETY," "ORDER" were the first injunctions issued by the committees; to which, on the suggestion of Mr. Hunt, was subsequently added that of

"PEACE." The fulfilment of the two first was left to the good sense of those who intended to join our procession to this "grand meeting"; the observance of the third and of the last injunctions,—ORDER, PEACE,—were provided for by general regulations. Order in our movements was obtained by drilling; and peace, on our parts, was secured, by a prohibition of all weapons of offence or defence; and by the strictest discipline, of silence, steadiness, and obedience to the directions of the conductors. Thus our arrangements, by constant practice, and an alert willingness, were soon rendered perfect, and ten thousand men moved with the regularity of ten score.

These drillings were also, to our sedentary weavers and spinners, periods of healthful exercise and enjoyment. Our drill masters were generally old soldiers of the line, or of militia, or local militia regiments; they put the lads through their facings in quick time, and soon learned them to march with a steadiness and regularity which would not have disgraced a regiment on parade. When dusk came, and we could no longer see to work, we jumped from our looms, and rushed to the sweet cool air of the fields, or the waste lands, or the green lane-sides. We mustered, we fell into rank, we faced, marched, halted, faced about, counter marched, halted again, dressed, and wheeled in quick succession, and without confusion. . . .

b) START OF THE MIDDLETON CONTINGENT

Our whole column with the Rochdale people would probably consist of 6,000 men. At our head were a hundred or two of women, mostly young wives, and my own was amongst them. A hundred or two of our handsomest girls—sweethearts to the lads who were with us—danced to the music or sang snatches of popular songs. . . . On each side of our line walked some thousands of stragglers. And thus, accompanied by our friends and our dearest and most tender connections we went slowly towards Manchester.

c) THE MASSACRE

The meeting was indeed a tremendous one. Hunt mounted the hustings; the music ceased. . . . Mr. Hunt, stepping towards the front of the stage, took off his white hat, and addressed the people.

Whilst he was doing so, I proposed to an acquaintance, that, as the speeches and resolutions were not likely to contain any thing new to us, and as we could see them in the papers, we should retire a while, and get some refreshment, of which I stood in much need, being in not very robust health. He assented, and we had got to nearly the outside of the crowd, when a noise and strange murmur arose towards the church. Some persons said it was the Blackburn people coming; and I stood on tip-toe, and looked in the direction whence the noise proceeded, and saw a party of cavalry in blue and white uniform, come trotting sword in hand, round the corner of a garden-wall, and to the front of a row of new houses, where they reined up in a line. . . .

On the cavalry drawing up they were received with a shout, of goodwill, as I understood it. They shouted again, waving their sabres over their heads; and then, slackening rein, and striking spur into their steeds, they dashed forward, and began cutting the people.

"Stand fast," I said, "they are riding upon us, stand fast." And there was a general cry in our quarter of "Stand fast." The cavalry were in confusion: they evidently could not, with all the weight of man and horse, penetrate that compact mass of human beings; and their sabres were plied to hew a way through naked held-up hands, and defenceless heads; and then chopped limbs, and wound-gaping skulls were seen; and groans and cries were mingled with the din of that horrid confusion. "Ah! ah!" "For shame! For shame!" was shouted. Then, "Break! break! they are killing them in front, and they cannot get away"; and there was a general cry of "Break! break." For a moment the crowd held back as in a pause; then was a rush, heavy and resistless as a headlong sea;

and a sound like low thunder, with screams, prayers, and imprecations from the crowd-moiled, and sabre doomed, who could not escape. . . .

On the breaking of the crowd, the yeomanry wheeled; and dashing wherever there was an opening, they followed, pressing and wounding. Many females appeared as the crowd opened; and striplings or mere youths also were found. Their cries were piteous and heart-rending; and would, one might have supposed, have disarmed any human resentment: but here their appeals were vain. Women, white-vested maids, and tender youths, were indiscriminately sabred or trampled. . . .

In ten minutes from the commencement of the havock, the field was an open and almost deserted space. The sun looked down through a sultry and motionless air. The curtains and blinds of the windows within view were all closed. A gentleman or two might occasionally be seen looking out from one of the new houses before-mentioned, near the door of which, a group of persons (special constables) were collected, and apparently in conversation; others were assisting the wounded, or carrying off the dead. The hustings remained, with a few broken and hewed flag-staves erect, and a torn and gashed banner or two dropping; whilst over the whole field, were strewed caps, bonnets, hats, shawls, and shoes, and other parts of male and female dress; trampled, torn and bloody. The yeomanry had dismounted,—some were easing their horses' girths, others adjusting their accoutrements; and some were wiping their sabres. Several mounds of human beings still remained where they had fallen, crushed down, and smothered. Some of these still groaning,— others with staring eyes, were gasping for breath, and others would never breathe more. All was silent save those low sounds, and the occasional snorting and pawing of steeds. Persons might sometimes be noticed peeping from attics and over the tall ridgings of houses, but they quickly withdrew, as if fearful of being observed, or unable to sustain the full gaze, of a scene so hideous and abhorrent.

Besides the Manchester yeomanry, who as I have already shewn, did "the duty of the day," there came upon the ground soon after the attack, the 15th hussars, and the Cheshire yeomanry; and the latter, as if emulous of the Manchester corps, intercepted the flying masses, and inflicted some severe sabre wounds. The hussars we have reason for supposing, gave but few wounds, and I am not aware that it has been shewn, that one of those brave soldiers dishonoured his sword by using the edge of it. In addition to the cavalry, a strong body of the 88th foot, was stationed at the lower corner of Dickinson-street: with their bayonets at the charge, they wounded several persons, and greatly impeded the escape of the fugitives by that out-let. Almost simultaneously with the hussars, four pieces of horse artillery appeared from Deansgate, and about two hundred special constables were also in attendance; so that, force for a thorough massacre was ready, had it been wanted.

On the first rush of the crowd, I called to our men to break their flag-staves, and secure their banners, but probably I was not heard, or understood, all being then, inextricable confusion. He with the blue banner, saved it, —the cap of liberty was dropped and left behind—indeed woe to him who stooped, he would never have risen again— and, Thomas Redford, who carried the green banner, held it aloft until the staff was cut in his hand, and his shoulder was divided by the sabre of one of the Manchester yeomanry.

A number of our people, were driven to some timber which lay at the foot of the wall of the Quakers' meeting house. Being pressed by the yeomanry, a number sprung over the balks and defended themselves with stones which they found there. It was not without difficulty, and after several were wounded, that they were driven out. A heroine, a young married woman of our party, with her face all bloody, her hair streaming about her, her bonnet hanging by the string, and her apron weighted with stones, kept her assailant at bay until she fell back-wards and was near being taken; but she got away covered with severe bruises. . . .

d) FRANCIS PLACE TO J. C. HOBHOUSE, AUGUST 20TH, 1819

. . . These Manchester yeomen and magistrates are a greater set of brutes than you form a conception of. They have always treated the working people in a most abominable manner. I know one of these fellows who swears, "Damn his eyes, 7/– a week is plenty for them"; that when he goes round to see how much work his weavers have in their looms, he takes a well-fed dog with him, almost, if not entirely for the purpose of, insulting them by the contrast. He said some time ago that "The sons of bitches had eaten up all the stinging nettles for 10 miles round Manchester, and now they had no greens to their broth." Upon my expressing indignation, he said, "Damn their eyes, what need you care about them? How could I sell you goods so cheap if I cared anything about them." I showed him the door, and never purchased any of his goods afterwards.

Another of these fellows, a manufacturer and yeoman, said yesterday, we in London did not know what a set of damned villains the fellows at Manchester were, they must be kept quiet by the sword. He was told to take care of himself; he laughed and said, "Ah, you know nothing of the weight of a sabre; that's the argument!" What but what has happened could be expected from these fellows when let loose. They never for a moment thought of consequences. They cut down and trampled down the people; and then it was to end just as cutting and trampling the furze bushes on a common would end. You may see what was thought of the transaction by the conduct of the fellow who hung the flag he had seized out of his window. The law will, from the want of proper interference, afford no redress. Should the people seek it by shooting their enemies one by one and burning their factories, I should not be at all surprised, nor much outraged. . . .

9. THE SIX GAG ACTS

From *Cobbett's Weekly Political Register*, January 6th, 1820.
The Fourth Act was specially directed against the cheap
edition of Cobbett's Register (see No. 2) and other working
class publications. Pamphlets and papers costing less than
6*d.* and appearing oftener than monthly were now liable to
the 4*d.* stamp tax on newspapers. Henry Hetherington
defied the regulation with his *Poor Man's Guardian* (see
No. 69), and in 1836 the tax was reduced to 1*d.*

THE struggle in which we have so long been engaged,
has now assumed a new aspect; and we must be prepared
for new exertions. . . . We have not proceeded in the way
of violence . . . we have maintained our rights by . . .
fair and solid argument. And how have we been answered?
The six Acts of Parliament, which have just been passed
contain the answer which we have received . . . the *first
of these Acts* is called the Training Act . . . any justice of
the peace, constable [etc.] . . . are empowered to disperse
men assembled for training, and to arrest and detain any
person present. . . .

The *second Act* . . . sets out by asserting that . . . arms
and weapons . . . have been collected and kept for purposes dangerous to the public peace . . . any justice of
the peace may issue his warrant for the seizure of any
such weapon. . . . Nay, I may be *laid hold of upon mere
suspicion of having such a weapon about me.* . . .

. . . The *third Act* . . . to restrain the use of the *tongue*
and of the *ears.* It commands that no meeting . . . exceeding the number of *fifty*, shall be held for the purpose . . .
of deliberating upon any public grievance . . . or upon
any matter in Church or State; or of considering any . . .
petition. . . . *But the ancient right of meeting to petition or
remonstrate is not to be done away!* Oh dear, no! By no
means! There are still to be meetings of counties, and of
cities, and of towns . . . to be called by the lords lieutenant;
the Sheriffs, the Mayors and so forth; and if they *do not
please* to call them, what then? Why, then, there are to

be no such meetings! But there still may be parish meetings. . . . Any justice of the peace who shall be present at the parish meeting, may order to be *taken into custody* anyone who shall . . . propose . . . any proposition for altering anything by law established, otherwise than by the authority of King, Lords, and Commons in Parliament assembled; or who shall . . . stir up the people to hatred or contempt of . . . *the Government and Constitution of this Realm as by law established.* . . . Magistrates . . . or any persons assisting them *may go to such meetings armed*; but nobody else is to attend with arms or weapons. . . . There are to be no flags or banners carried at such meetings. . . .

We may meet within doors to the amount of more than fifty . . . this Act prohibits . . . the taking of money for admission to such places unless . . . such places BE LICENCED BY TWO OR MORE JUSTICES OF THE PEACE . . . any justice of the peace may . . . at once take away the licence. . . .

The *fourth Act* is for stamping publications. . . .

The *fifth Act* introduces a new punishment for what are called libellers; and it authorises the seizing of libels already printed. It is called an Act for the more effectual prevention and punishment of blasphemous and seditious libels. . . .

Act the Sixth. Having, in the before-mentioned Acts, fitted us out pretty well with restraints, preventions, and punishments, it only remained to provide us with a speedy execution of the punishments; and this is pretty effectually done in the Act.

. . . It is quite sufficient to know that every printer, every bookseller, every publisher, every writer for the Press, is now liable to be banished, if he dare write, print, or publish anything which shall be regarded . . . as *tending* to bring into hatred or contempt, the *Government* and *Constitution . . . as by law established* . . . are we still to be told that we are free men? Good God Almighty! . . . Such is our situation at the end of the longest and most expensive war that nation ever knew . . . as the reward for . . . sacrifices we were promised a thousand times over, lasting prosperity, independence and freedom! . . . We were told that we were fighting *to secure the liberties of England, Scotland and Ireland* . . . and this is the reward; this is the consolation; this is the fruit of that war. . . . Despair, however, never yet did any good. . . . I am for making use of all the elbow-room, which we have yet left us by the Acts. . . .

10. THE CATO STREET CONSPIRACY, 1820

The conspiracy to murder the Tory Cabinet while at dinner in Cato Street, off Edgware Road, London, was, according to the leading participant, Arthur Thistlewood, instigated by a Home Office *agent provocateur*, who then, of course, exposed the whole affair. The use of such spies (No. 6) aroused the bitterest hatred in the Radical and Labour movement. Thistlewood was a prominent Spencean (No. 3). Extracts from his speech, after he was convicted of high treason, and the account of the execution are from *Cobbett's Weekly Political Register*, May 6th, 1820.

a) ARTHUR THISTLEWOOD'S SPEECH

I AM asked, my Lord, what I have to say that judgment of death should not be passed upon me. . . . This to me is a mockery for were the reasons I could offer incontrovertible . . . still would the vengeance of my lords Castlereagh and Sidmouth be satiated. . . . The reasons which I have, however, I will now state—not that I entertain the slightest hope from your sense of justice or from your pity. . . .

I protest against the proceedings upon my trial, which I consider to be grossly partial, and contrary to the very spirit of justice. . . . Ere the Solicitor-General replied to the address of my counsel, I applied to the Court to hear my witnesses. The court inhumanly refused. . . .

I would explain the motives which induced me to conspire against the ministers of his Majesty. . . . My every principle was for the prosperity of my country. My every feeling—the height of my ambition was the welfare of my starving countrymen . . . my feelings became too intense, too excessive for endurance, and I resolved on vengeance —I resolved that the lives of the instigators should be the requiem to the souls of the murdered innocents. . . . I was only wreaking national vengeance on a set of wretches unworthy the name or character of men.

. . . Edwards . . . a government spy . . . proposed a

plan for blowing up the House of Commons. This was
not my view—I wished to punish the guilty only, and
therefore I declined it. . . . He next proposed that we
should attack the ministers at the fete given by the
Spanish Ambassador. This I resolutely opposed because
the innocent would perish with the guilty. . . . Edwards
was ever at invention and at length he proposed attack-
ing them at a Cabinet dinner. . . . He, who was never
possessed of money to pay for a pint of beer, had always
plenty to purchase arms or ammunition. Amongst the
conspirators he was ever the most active . . . yet this
man . . . the entrapper, is screened from justice. . . .

. . . With respect to the immorality of our project, I will
just observe that the assassination of a tyrant has always
been deemed a meritorious action. . . . If the laws are
not strong enough to prevent them murdering the community, it becomes the duty of every member of that
community to rid his country of its oppressors. . . . Albion
is still in the chains of slavery—I quit it without regret
. . . I shall consider myself as murdered, if I am to be
executed on the verdict obtained against me, by the
refusal of the court to hear my evidence. . . . I seek not
pity: I demand but justice. . . .

b) EXECUTION OF THE PRISONERS

Mr. Thistlewood marched up to the . . . scaffold with
a composed countenance and bowed to the people . . .
he said, "I desire all to remember that I die in the cause
of liberty and that my last breath is given to that
cause. . . ."

Tidd said . . . "My poor wife. . . ." He behaved in the
most calm and firm manner.

Davidson appeared to pray. . . .

Ings jumped boldly up on the scaffold singing, "O give
me death or liberty." He gave three cheers which were
returned by the people. Seeing a newspaper reporter
taking notes, he said, "I die an enemy to tyrants. Write
down that, sir."

Brunt . . . saw the soldiers. "What," he exclaimed, "dare they not execute us without the aid of an army! . . ."

The people testified . . . by . . . hissing, groaning and by crying out "murder, murder, murder."

11. ARMED RESISTANCE, 1820

The following two documents illustrate attempts to organise armed resistance following the passage of the Six Gag Acts. Sixty thousand workers went on strike in Glasgow in March, 1820, and the movement spread rapidly. The military clashed with the insurgents at Bonnymuir, and many workers were wounded. Andrew Hardie was a forebear of Keir Hardie. Extracts are from the *Republican*, edited by Richard Carlile (No. 67): *a*) April 14th; *b*) September 22nd, 1820.

a) ADDRESS TO THE INHABITANTS OF GREAT BRITAIN AND IRELAND

ROUSED from that torpid state in which we have been sunk for so many years, we are at length compelled, from the extremity of our sufferings, and the contempt heaped upon our petitions for redress, to assert our rights at the hazard of our lives; and to proclaim . . . the real motives which . . . have induced us to take up arms for the redress of our common grievances. . . . Our principles are few, and founded on the basis of our constitution . . . equality of rights (not of property). . . . Liberty or death is our motto, and we have sworn to return home in triumph—or return no more!

Soldiers,—Shall you, countrymen, bound, by the sacred obligation of an oath, to defend your country and your King from enemies, whether foreign or domestic, plunge your bayonets into the bosoms of fathers and brothers, and at once sacrifice at the shrine of military despotism, to the unrelenting orders of a cruel faction, those feelings which you hold in common with the rest of mankind? Soldiers! turn your eyes towards Spain and there behold the happy effects resulting from the union of soldiers and citizens. . . . Come forward then at once, and free your country and your King from the power of those that have held them too, too long in thraldom. . . . The eventful period has now arrived . . . come forward . . . and sweep from our shores that corruption which has degraded us below the dignity of man. . . .

In the present state of affairs, and during the con-
tinuation of so momentous a struggle, we earnestly request
of all to desist from their labour, from and after this day,
the 1st of April; and attend wholly to the recovery of their
rights, and consider it as the duty of every man not to
recommence until he is in possession of those rights . . .
of giving consent to the laws by which he is to be
governed. . . .

And we hereby give notice to all those who shall
be found carrying arms against those who intend to
regenerate their country . . . we shall consider them as
traitors . . . and treat them as such.

*By order of the Committee of Organisation for forming a
Provisional Government, Glasgow, April 1st, 1820.*

b) THE BONNYMUIR REBELS

MORE LEGAL MURDER! EXECUTION OF BAIRD AND HARDIE
AT STIRLING. . . . These men, it will be recollected, were
two of the Bonnymuir combatants, who gallantly resisted
an escort of cavalry that was sent to take them prisoners.
They have been lately executed at Stirling by hanging
and beheading in the true British style. The papers of
Scotland expressed an astonishment at the composure of
the men, and the calm manner in which they took their
leave of the officers of Stirling castle. . . . Whilst Baird
was addressing the spectators, Hardie sat himself down
with perfect composure on the block prepared for the
decapitation, and when Baird had finished his address,
he arose in turn and began to address the spectators, just
as if he had been conducting the business of a public
meeting. The Sherriff or his depute tapped him on the
shoulder and bid him say something about religion.
Hardie was not to be alarmed, but shortened his address
by saying, *I die a martyr to the cause of liberty, truth and
justice.* This expression drew forth from the spectators as
enthusiastic a cheer, as if it had been a public meeting
for petition and remonstrance. . . . Both of them urged
the rectitude of their political principles and did not

express the least sorrow for what they had done. Much disapprobation and execration was expressed at the act of decapitation, and this brutal mangling seems to be continued as an emblem of the barbarity of the British government. Thus died two brave men, whose zeal for liberty was their only crime. . . .

Part Two

TRADE UNION ACTION AND THEORY

12. REPEAL OF THE COMBINATION LAWS,
1824

The evidence given before the Committee on Artisans and Machinery, 1824, led to the repeal of the 1799 laws which had made Trade Unions illegal. Extracts follow.

March 1st, 1824

Mr. George Ravenhill, called in; and Examined.

In what line of business are you?—A hat manufacturer.

Have you been long in that business?—Yes; I have been a partner in the house in which I am interested at present, about ten years.

During that time, have you found it necessary to unite with other master hat makers, with a view to regulate the price to be given to the workmen?—Yes, we have occasionally had meetings for the purpose of regulating the wages.

Have you ever had any prosecutions against you, by the men, for meetings of that kind?—Not within my recollection. . . .

Was the object of those meetings of the master hatters, to reduce the amount of wages claimed by the men?— The men at that time asked for an advance of wages above the prices that were given, and the masters thought the advance asked was extravagant, and they met for the purpose of regulating the price of wages, and then this new list was adopted, which was afterwards altered; making an increase on some particular sorts of hats. . . .

Do you not know that the object of writing to the masters in Gloucestershire was, that they should act in union with you in London, in carrying into effect the resolutions you had agreed to in June?—Probably it might have this intention. . . .

Were there any measures taken against the men, to prosecute any of them for holding out?—There were by some of the masters. . . .

To the best of your recollection, state what did pass with respect to prosecuting the men?—I believe, as far as I can recollect it, that the masters considered the combination, on the part of the journeymen, to be illegal, and that they in consequence determined to prosecute the men for the combination.

Did they agree to do it at the joint expense of all those present, or of the trade?—At the expense of the masters who were in the habit of attending the meetings at that time. . . .

Then you and the other masters acted under the impression, that it was legal for you to combine to prosecute the men for demanding higher wages, though it was not legal for the men to combine to demand higher wages?— That, I believe, was the impression on the minds of the masters. . . .

March 19th, 1824

Mr. Roger Fisher (Ship builder, Liverpool).

. . . Have you considered the effects of the Combination Laws in the disputes between you and the men?—I have, a little.

Have you considered them sufficient to prevent the combinations which have taken place?—I do not know what may be the cause, but the men are very bad to regulate; I think something might be done between masters and men, by leaving it to three indifferent magistrates in Liverpool, for instance, to fix between masters and men, I should think neither masters nor men would object to anything of that kind; if it could be done in that way, we should be glad; we do not like eternal disputes with our men.

Do you mean to say, that the present laws are not sufficient to enable you to settle your differences?—They are not effectual.

Do you think it would be better to repeal those laws, and leave the masters and men to make what bargain they choose?—I very much doubt it.

Do you think you should be better, or worse off, if

they were repealed?—I think the same combinations would go on then.

Do you not think, that where differences took place, the masters and men would meet each other, and come to an understanding?—No; the working classes are too systematic in their combinations.

May not that systematic arrangement have been to protect themselves against their masters?—It may have arisen so; but I think it will continue.

Do you know, from your intercourse with the men, whether they consider the Combination Laws as rather favourable to the masters, and against themselves?—Yes, I think they do.

Thinking as they do, are they not obliged to combine, to protect themselves against this supposed inequality of the law?—Yes, I suppose so.

Do not you think that if the laws were repealed, and you both left equal, a better understanding would subsist between you?—I am afraid not.

Why do you think so?—Because the clubs would still hold together, and the same thing would go on, in my opinion.

You admit that the men think the laws are against them?—Yes.

Do you not think that the men continue to keep up those clubs to protect themselves?—It may be so. . . .

March 23rd, 1824

Benjamin Taylor (Framework knitter, Nottingham).
. . . What is the general opinion in your trade, with respect to the operation of the Combination Laws; are they considered fair between man and man?—They are not, they are considered partial on the side of the masters; too favourable to them, and operating too much against the workmen.

Would it give general satisfaction if these laws were repealed?—It would.

Would the men be pleased to be left to make such

bargains with the masters as they might think proper?—
Yes, they would.

. . . Is it the opinion of the trade generally, that your
wages have been kept down in consequence of the Combination Laws?—It is; that is the universal opinion, from
one end of the trade to the other.

Have they never considered, that the briskness or dull-
ness of trade must operate on the rate of wages?—Yes,
they have; but when we have been as fully employed as
we possibly could, we never find the manufacturers very
willing to advance our wages. It is supposed there never
was a greater demand than now, but there is continually
one or other trying to lower the wages.

Are you individually now afraid of uniting to concert
any measure to oblige the masters to raise the wages
during this brisk state?—We have not been generally
much afraid of it, for we have advertised it at times; but
still we know that we are open to conviction. . . .

13. BACKGROUND OF THE TRADE UNION ACT, 1825

The great outbreak of strikes which followed the repeal of the Combination Laws in 1824 (No. 12) resulted in a further Government Committee and its consequence, the Trade Union Act of 1825. This left trade unions legal, but was designed to make almost any form of action a criminal offence. For nearly two generations, till the 'seventies, the struggle for the rights of trade union action continued. Extracts from Place's account, in the Place Papers, British Museum, Add. MSS. 27,798. For Place, see No. 8.

. . . THE [shipwrights] complained of certain obnoxious proceedings of their employers, of breach of contract, and want of regularity in the prices paid for their labour. They did not desire any advance of wages, but requested a conference for the purposes of regulation. This was peremptorily refused, and the men struck. The [employers] then came to a resolution not again to employ any man who belonged to the Shipwrights' Union. Disputes had been going on for some time amongst the sailors and Ship Owners, but the conduct of both the Sailors and Shipwrights was exemplary, no disorderly acts could be alleged against them, but as the Shipping interest, as it is called, had the ready ear of Ministers, they most shamefully misrepresented the conduct of the men, and represented the consequences as likely to lead to the destruction of the Commerce and Shipping of the Empire. Ministers were so ignorant as to be misled by these misrepresentations, and were mean and despicable enough to plot with these people against their workmen.

The interest of the unprincipled proprietors of the Times Newspaper was intimately connected with the "Shipping interest," and it lent its best services to their cause, it stuck at nothing in the way of false assertion and invective. It represented the conduct of Mr. Hume as mischievous in the extreme, and that of the working people all over the country as perfectly nefarious, and it urged ministers to re-enact the old laws, or to enact new ones, to bring the people into a state of miserable subjection.

In this state were matters when the Parliament assembled . . . in a few days, Mr. Huskisson gave notice that he should on the morrow move for a Committee on the Act of the last session (Mr. Hume's Act). . . .

In the Committee of 1824 every case was made as public as possible. In this Committee great pains were taken that nothing which passed in the Committee should be known, but they were all pains to no purpose. . . .

The working people of Dublin and Glasgow were accused of serious crimes. These accusations were recorded by the committee, and intended to be laid before the House. Still the Committee would hear none of the persons whom it was desirable should have been sent from these places to rebut the accusations. Men's names were used, as having in Glasgow abetted murder, and yet, notwithstanding the very men who had been so named wrote to Mr. Hume and to the Chairman of the Committee requesting to be examined, the Committee persisted in refusing to hear them. The men said, "We are men of good character, have done no wrong to anyone, are at work in the same shops and factories in which we have worked for years, and have nothing objected to us by our employers; we demand the opportunity to clear ourselves from the imputation." But no, the Committee would not hear them; it would record the accusation, add the weight of its authority to it, and leave the accused without a defence. Mr. Huskisson was base enough to call the men thus accused, and thus refused a hearing, "*Acquitted Felons*"; and yet they were *unacquitted*, for they had been accused only before the Committee, who had not condescended to do either them or themselves the justice of trying them at the bar of the Committee.

Notwithstanding this, no one was refused a hearing who came with a complaint against the workmen; no one was refused payment for his time and travelling expenses who gave evidence against the men, while many of the men who had been weeks in attendance, and were at length forced on the notice of the Committee and were examined by them, were refused any remuneration whatsoever. . . .

These were the notions these wise men entertained of justice. The masters might consult when and where they pleased; give what instructions they pleased; have the ears of members of the Committee, and go in and out of the Committee-room while the Committee was sitting as often as they pleased. But the workmen were to have no one to assist them; no one was to instruct them, notwithstanding they were the party who most needed instruction. . . .

14. *LABOUR DEFENDED*

Thomas Hodgskin (1783–1869), naval officer turned journalist and economist, was one of the founders of the London Mechanics Institution (later Birkbeck College, University of London). His anti-capitalist lectures and books, of which *Labour Defended* is the best known, exercised a great influence on many who were later to become prominent leaders of the working-class movement, e.g. Henry Hetherington, William Lovett and Bronterre O'Brien, and were well studied by Marx (see Introduction, p. 20). Hodgskin applied his "labour theory of value" to the defence of trade unions when the repeal of the Combination Laws was in question. Extracts below are from *Labour Defended against the Claims of Capital; or The Unproductiveness of Capital proved with Reference to the Present Combinations amongst Journeymen*, 1825, edited by G. D. H. Cole, 1922, pp. 60, 63–6, 71–7, 101–5.

. . . ONE is almost tempted to believe that capital is a sort of cabalistic word, like Church or State, or any other of those general terms which are invented by those who fleece the rest of mankind to conceal the hand that shears them. . . .

For a nation to have fixed capital, then, and to make a good use of it . . . only three things seem to me to be requisite. First, knowledge and ingenuity for inventing machines. No labourer would, I am sure, be disposed to deny these their reward. But no subject of complaint is more general or more just than that the inventor of any machine does not reap the benefit of it. . . . Thousands of capitalists have been enriched by inventions and discoveries of which they were not the authors, and capital, by robbing the inventor of his just reward, is guilty of stifling genius. The second requisite for having fixed capital is the manual skill and dexterity for carrying these inventions into execution. The third requisite is the skill and labour to use these instruments after they are made. Without knowledge they could not be invented, without manual skill and dexterity they could not be made, and without skill and labour they could not be productively used. But there is nothing more than the knowledge, skill and labour requisite, on which the capitalist can found a claim to any share of the produce.

Naturally and individually man is one of the most feeble and destitute of all created animals. His intelligence, however, compensates for his physical inferiority . . . he presses all the elements into his service, and makes Nature herself the handmaid to his will. The instruments he uses to do all this, which have been invented by his intelligence to aid his feeble powers, and which are employed by his skill and by his hands, have been called fixed capital; and shutting out of view MAN himself, in order to justify the existing order of society, which is founded on property or possessions, and the existing oppression of the labourer, who forms unhappily part of these possessions—all these glorious effects have been attributed with a more extraordinary perversion of thought, perhaps, than is to be found in any other department of knowledge, to fixed and circulating capital. The skill and the art of the labourer have been overlooked and vilified while the work of his hands has been worshipped. . . .

Betwixt him who produces food and him who produces clothing, betwixt him who makes instruments and him who uses them, in steps the capitalist, who neither makes nor uses them and appropriates to himself the produce of both. With as niggard a hand as possible he transfers to each a part of the produce of the other, keeping to himself the larger share. Gradually and successively has he insinuated himself betwixt them, expanding in bulk as he has been nourished by their increasingly productive labours, and separating them so widely from each other that neither can see whence that supply is drawn which each receives through the capitalist. While he despoils both, so completely does he exclude one from the view of the other that both believe they are indebted to him for subsistence. He is the *middleman* of all labourers; and when we compare what the skilled labour of England produces, with the produce of the untutored labour of the Irish peasantry, the middlemen of England cannot be considered as inferior in their exactions to the middlemen of Ireland. They have been more fortunate, however, and while the latter are stigmatised as oppressors, the former are honoured as benefactors. Not only do they appropriate the produce of the labourer; but they have succeeded in persuading him that they are his benefactors and employers. At least such are the doctrines of political economy; and capitalists may well be pleased with a science which both justifies their claims and holds them up to our admiration, as the great means of civilising and improving the world. . . .

Perhaps I can make the evil effects of capital more apparent by another sort of example. The *real price* of a coat or a pair of shoes or a loaf of bread, *all* which nature demands from man in order that he may have either of these very useful articles, is a certain quantity of labour; how much it is almost impossible to say, from the manufacture of a coat, a pair of shoes or a loaf of bread, being completed by many persons. But for the *labourer* to have either of these articles he must give over and above the quantity of labour nature demands from him, a still larger quantity to the capitalist. . . .

. . . before a labourer can have a loaf of bread he must give a quantity of labour more than the loaf costs, by all that quantity which pays the profit of the farmer, the corn dealer, the miller and the baker, with profit on all the buildings they use; and he must moreover pay with the produce of his labour the rent of the landlord. How much more labour a LABOURER must give to have a loaf of bread than that loaf costs, it is impossible for me to say. I should probably underrate it were I to state it at six times; or were I to say that the real cost of that loaf, for which the labourer must give sixpence, is one penny. Of this, however, I am quite certain, that the Corn Laws, execrable as they are in principle, and mischievous as they are to the whole community, do not impose anything like so heavy a tax on the labourer as capital. Indeed, however injurious they may be to the capitalist, it may be doubted whether they are so to the labourer. Whether there are Corn Laws or not, the capitalist must allow the labourer to subsist, and as long as his claims are granted and acted on he will never allow him to do more. . . .

The interest of the different classes of labourers who are now first beginning to think and act as a body, in opposition to the other classes among whom, with themselves, the produce of the earth is distributed, and who are now only for the first time beginning to acquire as extensive a knowledge of the principles of government as those who rule, is too deeply implicated by these principles to allow them to stop short in their career of inquiry. They may care nothing about the curious researches of the geologist or the elaborate classification of the botanist, but they will assuredly ascertain *why* they only out of all classes of society have always been involved in poverty and distress. They will not stop short of any ultimate truth, and they have experienced too few of the advantages of society to make them feel satisfied with the present order of things. The mind is rather invigorated than enfeebled by the labour of the hands; they will carry forward their investigations undelayed by the pedantry of learning, and undiverted by the fastidiousness of taste.

By casting aside the prejudices which fetter the minds of those who have benefited by their degradation, they have everything to hope. On the other hand, they are the sufferers by these prejudices, and have everything to dread from their continuance. Having no reason to love those institutions which limit the reward of labour, whatever may be its produce, to a bare subsistence, they will not spare them, whenever they see the hollowness of the claims made on their respect. As the labourers acquire knowledge, the foundations of the social edifice will be dug up from the deep beds into which they were laid in times past, they will be curiously handled and closely examined, and they will not be restored unless they were originally laid in justice, and unless justice commands their preservation. . . .

In truth, also, however the matter may be disguised, the combinations among workmen to obtain higher wages, which are now so general and so much complained of, are practical attacks on the claims of capital. The weight of its chains are felt, though the hand may not yet be clearly felt which imposes them. Gradually as the resistance increases, as laws are multiplied for the protection of capital, as claims for higher wages shall be more strenuously and more violently repressed, the cause of this oppression will be more distinctly seen. The contest now appears to be between masters and journeymen, or between one species of labour and another, but it will soon be displayed in its proper characters; and will stand confessed a war of honest industry against the idle profligacy which has so long ruled the affairs of the political world with undisputed authority—which has, for its own security, added honour and political power to wealth, and has conjoined exclusion and disgrace with the poverty it has inflicted on the labourer. On the side of the labourers there is physical strength, for they are more numerous than their opponents. They are also fast losing that reverence for their opponents which was and is the source of their power, and they are daily acquiring a moral strength which results from a common interest and a close and intimate union.

The capitalists and labourers form the great majority of the nation, so that there is no third power to intervene betwixt them. They must and will decide the dispute of themselves. Final success, I would fain hope, must be on the side of justice. I am certain, however, that till the triumph of labour be complete; till productive industry alone be opulent, and till idleness alone be poor, till the admirable maxim that "he who sows shall reap" be solidly established; till the right of property shall be founded on principles of justice, and not on those of slavery; till *man* shall be held more in honour than the clod he treads on, or the machine he guides—there cannot, and there ought not to be either peace on earth or goodwill amongst men.

15. SUPERIORITY OF CO-OPERATION:
W. THOMPSON, 1824

William Thompson (1783–1833) was a landowner who
became a fervent supporter of Owen's principles of Socialism
and co-operation. Extract *a*) is from Thompson's *Inquiry into
the Principle of the Distribution of Wealth Most Conducive to
Human Happiness*, 1824, pp. 582–4, 590–7; *b*) is from his
Labor Rewarded, 1827, pp. 97–8, which was a reply to
Hodgskin's *Labour Defended*.

a) OUR object being, to ascertain that mode of distributing
wealth which would lead to its greatest reproduction and
to the greatest preponderant happiness from all other
sources; all former modes of production and distribution
have . . . been . . . used simply as materials to enable us
to form that judgement aright. . . . Men, labor, materials.
. . . How out of these to fabricate the greatest mass of
happiness which wealth affords . . .? It was found at the
beginning of the inquiry that *equality* of distribution was
calculated to produce incalculably more happiness than
any other mode of distributing wealth . . . provided such
distribution were effected without the evils of force. . . .
Equality must be limited by security. Security means
"free labor, entire use of its products, and voluntary
exchanges." Without security there is no reproduction.
. . . The security . . . spoken of is the equal security for
all, not the security of a few only. . . .

. . . equality and security equally demand . . . that
every producer of wealth shall have the entire use of the
products of his labor or exertion. But as long as the
laborer . . . possesses neither the tools nor the machinery
to work with, the land or the materials to work upon,
. . . so long will he remain deprived of almost all the
products of his labor. . . . A strict adherence for the
future to the natural laws of distribution, free labor,
entire use of its products and voluntary exchange . . .
would . . . gradually put all productive laborers in

possession of the several articles, under the name of capital, which are necessary to them to enable them to gather the fruits of their industry.

But . . . there are two modes of production which may be employed to attain this most essential object. . . . It is . . . inconsistent with human happiness . . . that capital should be possessed by one set of individuals and labor by another. Utility demands that all productive laborers should become capitalists, that labor and capital should be in the same hands. . . .

The two modes . . . of effecting this union are,

The mode of production by labor, with equal individual competition. The mode of production by labor with mutual co-operation.

. . . The advantages of the system of labor by mutual co-operation over the best direction of it by individual exertion have been explained . . . enough to show the great superiority of that mode of production, not only as respects wealth but every other source of happiness. . . .

As long as the accumulated capital of society remains in one set of hands, and the productive powers of creating wealth remain in another, this accumulated capital will . . . be made use of to counteract the natural laws of distribution and to deprive the producers of the use of what their labor has produced. . . . As long as a class of mere capitalists exists, society must remain in a diseased state. Whatever plunder is saved from the hand of political power, will be levied in another way under the name of profits, by capitalists, who, while capitalists must always be the law makers. . . .

. . . The system of labor by mutual co-operation . . . can well afford a competition with individual . . . exertion. . . . Equal Security once established . . . the real superiority of labor by co-operation will be apparent . . . a theatre boundless as human efforts will be opened to every possible combination of labor . . . the co-operating communities . . . may exert all their energies and multiply their productions in peace, assured that the whole fruits of their industry will be at their own disposal.

b) The author of the pamphlet *Labour Defended* stands alone, as far as I know, amongst the advocates of Individual Competition, in even *wishing* that labor should possess the whole of the products of its exertion. All other advocates of Individual Competition look on the notion as visionary, under the Competitive System. I think with them that the possession by Labor of the whole products of its exertions, is incompatible with individual competition. . . . The sole means which *Labour Defended* points out to accomplish the great object . . . is the withholding from the mere possessors of capital . . . any part of the products of labor. The author does not propose to accomplish this by force. . . . He admits . . . that [no] means, can . . . under the complicated system of industry point out *what are*, what proportions of the value of any article are, the products of the labor of any individual laborer. He thus admits the impossibility of accomplishing his favourite object under the system of Individual Competition. . . . It is surely incumbent on him, either to relinquish this object or to devise some means by which . . . it can be accomplished; or failing that, to advocate the only system of industry yet devised by which . . . *large numbers* of associated laborers may possess and enjoy the whole products of their united labor, the system of Mutual Co-operation (universal insurance) and Equal Distribution.

16. A UNION OF ALL TRADES, 1830

John Doherty (born 1799), leader of the Lancashire cotton workers, was outstanding in all the working-class agitations of the period. Organiser of the first national Trades Union, described below, he edited (1) *The Voice of the People*; (2) *The Poor Man's Advocate*; (3) *The Herald of the Rights of Industry*; all of which made a great contribution to trade unionism, and the fight for the shorter working day (see No. 64). The extracts are from the *Address of the National Association for the Protection of Labour. To the Workmen of the United Kingdom*, 1830 (pamphlet in the Goldsmiths' Library, University of London).

FELLOW WORKERS,—The fearful change, which the workings of the last few years have produced in the condition of every class of labourers, summons you to a serious investigation of the cause. It warns you that the time is now come for you to make a stand . . . in your downward course to . . . pauperism. . . . Your power, as regards the operations of society, is omnipotent . . . there is no moment in which you may not burst the strongest chain that tyrants ever forged to bind you. You are the great lever by which everything is effected. The erection of palaces, factories, dungeons . . . the construction of ships . . . you comprise the armies . . . your labour furnishes "the sinews of war." . . . Let British operatives once become firm and united, and their unanimous voice of complaint will command respect. . . . Of all the causes which have conspired to reduce you to what you are . . . reduction of wages stands foremost, and claims your first attention. . . . Time after time has the Government been appealed to for protection. That protection was denied you. . . . The only mode hitherto adopted for preventing reductions of wages has been by partial unions of individual trades. . . . The United States . . . knew that union, in order to be successful, must be general. . . . This, then, is the principle which we propose to the workmen of the United Kingdom—*a union of all trades*—

this is the principle upon which 80,000 men, who have already joined the Union, have agreed to act. . . .

To those who have embarked in schemes of co-operation we beg to point out the imperative necessity for their supporting the National Union. . . .

The National Association has . . . established . . . *The United Trades Journal*, to support the interests and defend the rights of workmen. . . .

. . . It only remains for us to ask the workmen of the United Kingdom, of every trade and calling, whether they are prepared to crown with their sanction this spirited attempt to retrieve them from degradation. . . . Let us not, henceforth, be taunted with the assertion that "Unions have failed." Here we offer a Union which has never yet been tried . . . suffer no paltry jealousies to stop or divide you in this great national struggle for the recovery and maintenance of your rights. And do not, when all others are united against you, weaken or destroy your own force by disunion and division. . . .

Secretary, Mr. John Doherty . . . Manchester.

17. THE GENERAL STRIKE

William Benbow (1784?-*c.* 1850) is a name that recurs in all the agitations of the twenty-five years after Waterloo. Printer, publisher, coffee-house proprietor, he served at least two sentences of imprisonment for his working-class activities. The pamphlet quoted here was widely circulated, and its influence is apparent in speeches of contemporary working-class agitators. It was the first exposition of a general strike theory. The extracts are from *Grand National Holiday and Congress of the Productive Classes, etc.*, by William Benbow, 1832.

A HOLIDAY signifies a *holy* day, and ours is to be of holy days the most holy. It is to be most holy, most sacred, for it is to be consecrated to promote—to create rather—the happiness and liberty of mankind. Our holy day is established to establish plenty, to abolish want, to render all men equal! In our holy day we shall legislate for all mankind; the constitution drawn up during our holiday shall place every human being on the same footing. Equal rights, equal liberties, equal enjoyments, equal toil, equal respect, equal share of production: this is the object of our holy day—of our sacred day,—of our festival! . . .

The grounds and necessity of our having a month's Holiday, arise from the circumstances in which we are placed. We are oppressed in the fullest sense of the word; we have been deprived of everything; we have no property, no wealth, and our labour is of no use to us, since what it produces goes into the hands of others. . . .

. . . One scoundrel, one sacrilegious blasphemous scoundrel, says "that over production is the cause of our wretchedness." Over production, indeed! when we half-starving producers cannot, with all our toil, obtain anything like a sufficiency of produce. It is the first time, that in any age or country, save our own, *abundance* was adduced as a cause of *want*. Good God! where is this abundance? Abundance of food! ask the labourer and mechanic where they find it. Their emaciated frame is the best answer. Abundance of clothing! the nakedness, the shivering, the asthmas, the colds, and rheumatisms of the people, are proofs of the abundance of clothing! Our Lords and Masters tell us, we produce too much; very well then, we shall cease from producing for one month, and thus put into practice the theory of our Lords and Masters. . . .

. . . In our National Holiday, which is to be held during one calendar month, throughout the United Kingdom of Great Britain and Ireland, we must all unite in discovering the source of our misery, and the best way of destroying it. Afterwards we must choose, appoint, and send to the place of Congress, a certain number of wise and cunning men, whom we shall have made full acquainted with our circumstances; and they, before the Holiday be expired, shall discuss and concert a plan, whereby, if it is possible, the privation, wretchedness, and slavery, of the great mass of us, may be diminished, if not completely annihilated. . . .

. . . We shall then by our consultations, deliberations, discussions, holiday and congress, endeavour to establish the happiness of the *immense majority* of the human race, of that *far largest* portion called *the working classes*. What the few have done for themselves, cannot the many do for themselves? unquestionably. Behold, O people and fellow labourers, the way! . . .

Committees of management of the working classes must be forthwith formed in every city, town, village, and parish throughout the United Kingdom. These committees must make themselves fully acquainted with the plan, and be determined to use the extremest activity and perseverance to put it into execution as speedily and effectually as possible. They must call frequent meetings, and shew the necessity and object of the holiday. . . .

We suppose that the people are able to provide provisions and funds for one week; during this week they will be enabled to enquire into the funds of their respective cities, towns, villages and parishes, and to adopt means of having those funds, originally destined for their benefit, now applied to that purpose. The committee of management shall be required to direct the people in adopting the best measures that shall be deemed necessary. . . .

The committee, which may also be looked upon as the commissary department, must likewise watch over the good order of its district, establish regularity, and punish all attempts at disorder. The people having a grand object in view, the slightest points in their character must be grand. About to renovate Europe, the people must appear renovated. . . .

When all the details of the above plan are put into execution, the committee of each parish and district, shall select its wise men to send to the NATIONAL CONGRESS. A parish or district having a population of 8,000, shall send two wise and cunning men to Congress, a population of 15,000 four, a population of 25,000 eight, and London fifty wise and cunning men. . . .

The object of the Congress; that is what it will have to do. To reform society, for "from the crown of our head to the sole of our foot there is no soundness in us." We must cut out the rottenness in order to become sound. Let us see what is rotten. Every man that does not work is rotten; he must be made to work in order to cure his unsoundness. Not only is society rotten; but the land, property, and capital is rotting. There is not only something, but a great deal rotten in the state of England. Everything, man, property, and money, must be put into a state of circulation. As the blood by stagnation putrifies, as it is impoverished by too much agitation, so society by too much idleness on the one hand, and too much toil on the other, has become rotten. Every portion must be made to work, and then the work will become so light, that it will not be considered work, but wholesome exercise. Can anything be more humane than the main object of our glorious holiday, namely, to obtain for all at the least expense to all, the largest sum of happiness for all. . . .

18. ON THE SPREAD OF TRADES UNIONISM, 1833

See Introduction, p. 23, for the developments in trade unionism after the disillusion of the Reform Act, 1832. The extract is from the *Poor Man's Guardian*, October 19th, 1833. For this paper, see No. 69.

. . . *a spirit of combination has grown up among the working classes, of which there has been no example in former times.* A grand national organisation, which promises to embody the physical power of the country, is silently, but rapidly progressing; and the object of it is the sublimest that can be conceived, namely—*to establish for the productive classes a complete dominion over the fruits of their own industry.* Heretofore, these classes have wasted their strength in fruitless squabbles with their employers, or with one another. They have never sought any grand object, nor have they been united for those they sought. To obtain some paltry rise, or prevent some paltry reduction in wages, has been the general aim of their turn-outs; and the best result of their best combinations, even when successful, was merely to secure their members against actual want in the day of sickness, or of superannuation. These and the like objects were only worthy of slaves; they did not strike at the root of the evil; they did not aim at any radical change; their tendency was not to alter the system, but rather to perpetuate it, by rendering it more tolerable; nay, they in some respects only aggravate the evils of the workman's condition, as for instance, in benefit societies, of which the tendency is to pinch the bellies and backs of the contributors to the fund, in order to save the poor-rates, that is to say, the pockets of the affluent classes, from the just claims of broken-down industry. . . . But far different from the paltry objects of all former combinations is that now aimed at . . . reports show that an entire change in society—a change amounting to a complete subversion of the existing "order of the world"—is contemplated by the working classes. They aspire to be at the top instead of at the bottom of society—or rather that there should be no bottom or top at all!

19. THE BUILDERS' UNION, 1832-4

Extract *a*) is from *Character, Object and Effects of Trades Unions*, by Edward Tuffnell, 1834; *b*) which illustrates the influence on the unions of Owen's ideas, is from the Co-operative Union Records, Manchester (Miscellaneous Correspondence); *c*) is a specimen of the masters' "document" (signature to which was made a condition of employment) from the *Brief History of the Proceedings of the Operative Builders' Trades Unions*, 1833; *b*) and *c*) are quoted from *The Builders' History*, by R. W. Postgate, 1923.

a) AN OATH

I DO, before Almighty God and this Loyal Lodge, most solemnly swear, that I will not work for any master that is not in the union, nor will I work with any illegal man or men, but will do my best for the support of wages; and most solemnly swear to keep inviolate all the secrets of this Order; nor will I ever consent to have any money for any purpose but for the use of the Lodge and the support of the trade; nor will I write or cause to be wrote, print, mark, either on stone, marble, brass, paper, or sand, anything connected with this Order, so help me God, and keep me steadfast in this my present obligation; and I further promise to do my best to bring all legal men that I am connected with into this Order; and if I ever reveal any of the rules, may what is before me plunge my soul into eternity.

b) OPERATIVE BUILDERS' UNION MANIFESTO, 1833

. . . we have formed ourselves into a National Building Guild of Brothers, to enable us to erect buildings of every description upon the most extensive scale in England, Scotland and Ireland.

By the arrangement and organisation which we have adopted we shall accomplish the following important results,

1st.—We shall be enabled to erect all manner of dwellings and other architectural designs for the public more expeditiously, substantially and economically than any Masters can build them under the individual system of competition.

2nd.—We shall be enabled to withdraw all our Brethren of the National Builders Guild and their Families from being a burden upon the public, for they will be supported in old age, infancy, sickness or infirmity of any kind from the general funds of the Guild.

3rd.—None of the Brethren will be unemployed when they desire to work, for when the public do not require their services they will be employed by the Guild to erect superior dwellings and other buildings for themselves, under superior arrangements, that they, their wives and their children may live continuously surrounded by those virtuous external circumstances which alone can form an intelligent, prosperous, good and happy population.

4th.—We shall be enabled to determine upon a just and equitable remuneration or wages for the services of the Brethren according to their skill and conduct when employed by the public.

5th.—We shall also be placed in a position to decide upon the amount of work or service to be performed, each day, by the Brethren, in order that none may be oppressed by labour beyond their powers of body or mind.

6th.—We shall be enabled to form arrangements in all parts of the British dominions to re-educate all our adult Brethren that they may enjoy a superior mode of existence, by acquiring new and better dispositions, habits, manners language and conduct, in order that they may become such examples for their children as are requisite to do justice to all young persons whose characters are to be formed to become good practical members of society.

7th.—We shall form arrangements, as soon as circumstances admit, to place all the children of the Brethren, under such instruction of persons and influences of external objects as shall train or educate the *will, inclination and powers* within each to induce and enable them to become better Architects and Builders of the human character, intellectually and morally than the world has yet known or even deemed to be practicable.

8th.—We will form arrangements to enable all other classes of Producers of real wealth to unite with us to obtain equal advantages for themselves, their children and their children's children to the end of time.

9th.—We will exhibit to the world, in a plain and simple manner, by our quiet example, how easily the most valuable wealth may be produced in superfluity beyond the wants of the population of all countries; also how beneficially for the Producing Classes (and all classes will soon perceive their interest on becoming superior producers) the present artificial, inaccurate and therefore injurious circulating medium for the exchange of our riches, may be superceded by an equitable, accurate and therefore rational representation of real wealth, and as a consequence of these important advances in true civilization, how beautifully, yet how accurately the causes which generate the bad passions and all the vices and corruptions attributed to human nature, shall gradually diminish until they all die a natural death and be known no more, except as matter of past history, and thus by contrast, be the cause for everlasting rejoicing.

10th.—We shall by these and other means now easy of adopting speedily open the road to remove the causes of individual and national competition, of individual and national contest, jealousies and wars, and enable all to discover their true individual interests and thereby establish peace, goodwill and harmony, not only among the Brethren of the Building Guild, but also by their example among the human race for ever.

11th.—We shall secure to the present Masters of all the Building Branches who well understand their business a far more advantageous and secure position in Society than they have or can have under the system of individual competition between Master and Master and Man and Man, and we shall open the way to unite their interests cordially, firmly and permanently with the real body of the National Builders Guild.

12th.—We shall be enabled to exhibit by our new organisation and practical operations, the means by which the individual and general interests of the classes may be united and all be made gradually to become useful members of the great Association for the Emancipation of the Productive Classes.

c) THE "DOCUMENT"

We, the undersigned . . . do hereby declare that we are not in any way connected with the General Union of the Building Trades and that we do not and will not contribute to the support of such members of the said union as are or may be out of work in consequence of belonging to such union. June 15th, 1833.

20. THE GRAND NATIONAL CONSOLIDATED TRADES UNION, 1834

This historic organisation, which attracted over half a million members in a few months, reflected the influence upon the trade unions of Owen's theories of co-operative production. See also Nos. 19, 21, 22 b). The extract is from the Report of the Proceedings of a special meeting of Trades Union delegates in London, February 13th–19th, 1834, published in the *Pioneer*, March 8th, 1834. The editor of the *Pioneer* was James Morrison (*d.* 1835), a building worker, whose leading articles expounded the revolutionary trade unionism of the day. The *Pioneer* became the official paper of the G.N.C.T.U.

1. THAT as many different Trades Unions as possible do mutually agree under a perfect understanding with each other, to maintain a unity of action in all their proceedings with respect to their general laws and government, and also with regard to the levying and disposing of all funds raised for objects of presumed permanent utility.

2. As land is the source of the first necessaries of life, and as, without the possession of it, the producing classes will ever remain in a greater or less degree subservient to the money capitalists, and subject to the deterioration of the money value of their labour consequent upon the fluctuations of trade and commerce, this committee advise that a great effort should now be made by the Unions to secure such portions of it on lease as their funds will permit, in order that in all turn-outs the men may be employed in rearing the greater part, if not the whole, of their subsistence under the direction of practical agricultural superintendents, which arrangements would not have the effect of lowering the price of labour in any trade, but on the contrary would rather tend to increase it by drawing off the at present superfluous supply in manufactures. . . .

3. The committee would nevertheless, earnestly recommend in all cases of strikes and turn-outs, where it is

practicable, that the men be employed in the making or producing of all such commodities as would be in demand among their brother unionists; and that to effect this, each lodge should be provided with a workroom or shop in which these commodities may be manufactured on account of such lodge which shall make proper arrangements for the supply of the necessary materials.

4. That great advantages would accrue by the formation, in each district lodge, of a fund for the support of the sick and aged.

5. That in all cases where it be practicable, each district or branch lodge should establish one or more depots for provisions and articles in general domestic use; by which means the working man may be supplied with the best commodities at little above wholesale prices.

6. That each lodge do make arrangements for furnishing the means of mental improvement to their members, and for the cultivation of good habits among them, by affording them every facility for meeting together for friendly conversation, mutual instruction and rational amusement or recreation; which arrangements might be rendered in a short period infinitely more enticing and agreeable than the delusive, pernicious, and dearly-bought gratifications sought after in the tap-room or the gin-shop.

7. As a very large number of females among the industrious classes are exposed to great hardships we should offer [them] . . . every encouragement and assistance to form lodges for the protection of their industry.

A plan for the consolidation of the Unions was submitted and approved. . . . The preliminary Articles for establishing the Consolidated Union were agreed to and signed accordingly. . . .

21. TRADE UNION SOLIDARITY, 1833-4

Sources of extracts: *a*) *Pioneer*, December 21st, 1833; *b*) *The Crisis*, August 2nd, 1834; *c*) *Pioneer*, May 3rd, 1834; *d*) *Pioneer*, May 10th, 1834. *The Crisis* was Owen's "official" organ. Its editor, James E. Smith (1801-57), was also a remarkable lecturer, and exponent of utopian socialism. These extracts illustrate some of the conditions producing the outburst of unco-ordinated strikes during the short-lived existence of the G.N.C.T.U. between February and August, 1834.

a) THE DERBY LOCK-OUT

Committee of United Trades

To the whole of the Operatives of Birmingham, and the surrounding districts,—Fellow workmen,

We call upon you, at this momentous crisis, to . . . maintain your rights as workmen, and to put down a despotism which threatens to grind us to the very earth. At Derby, a combination of masters (leagued with all those who wish to keep us in poverty and ignorance), have sent forth their hateful decree, to starve into compliance the industrious poor, who have earned them their riches. . . . The plain matter of fact is this, that in Derby from 1,200 to 1,500 men, women, and children, are thrown out of employment for no other cause than that of peacefully uniting for their common good, and but for the assistance of their fellow workmen throughout the United Kingdom, they will be left to the mercy of these avaricious tyrants. . . . Fellow workmen,—Awake! arise! aid and assist, for their cause is our cause, and their hope is our hope.

The committee will sit every night from seven till ten o'clock, to receive donations, subscriptions and advice at the Town hall Tavern. . . . Dec. 10th, 1833.

b) GRAND LODGE OF OPERATIVE CORDWAINERS

Resolved, "That we, the Operative Cordwainers of

London, do pledge ourselves not to drink any Beer of
the firm of Combe Delafield and Co. until they withdraw their opposition from the 'Trades Unions,' and
that we will use our influence with all other trades to
the same."

W. Hoare, *General Secretary.*

July 28, 1834.

c) THE FRIENDLY SOCIETY OF OPERATIVE TAILORS (LONDON)

No brother shall work more than ten hours per day
from the third Monday in . . . April to the last Saturday
in . . . July; nor more than eight hours per day the
remaining eight months of the year; and for such labour
the remuneration shall be six shillings per day for the
ten hours labour, which is to be performed between the
hours of seven o'clock in the morning and six o'clock in
the evening; and five shillings per day for the eight hours
labour, to be performed between eight o'clock in the
morning and five o'clock in the evening out of which
time . . . he shall leave his employer's premises one hour
for refreshment. Nor shall any brother work for an
employer anywhere but on his (the employers) premises,
which shall be healthy and convenient, or on any other
terms than by the day or hour. . . .

d) OFFICIAL NOTICE

TO THE GRAND NATIONAL CONSOLIDATED TRADES' UNION

Whereas our brothers, the United Operative Tailors of
the Metropolis, being forced into their present position by
the many grievous attacks and encroachments of the
Masters, and we being fully aware of the great danger
and inconvenience of large masses of Men remaining in
idleness.

We do therefore require that all and every of the
members of the Consolidated Trades' Union do forthwith

contribute the sum of One Shilling and Sixpence as levy . . . for the purpose of giving employment to the members of the above Trade . . . it is desired that all Secretaries will see the said Money transmitted to

May 5 1834.   Mr. E. C. Douglas, 213, High Holborn.
By Order of the Executive Council,
God save the Union.

22. THE TOLPUDDLE MARTYRS, 1834

Extract *a*) is from *The Victims of Whiggery*, by George Loveless, 1837, written on his return from Tasmania in 1837, after the agitation for release of the "Martyrs" had secured a reduction of the original sentence of transportation. The movement of solidarity with the victims to achieve a reversal of the savage verdicts is described in *b*) from the *Pioneer*, April 26th, 1834, which gives an account of the great London demonstration in Copenhagen Fields, April 21st, 1834, organised by the Grand National Consolidated Union.

a) THE STORY OF THE DORCHESTER LABOURERS

. . . FROM this time we were reduced to seven shillings a week, and shortly after our employers told us they must lower us to six shillings per week. The labouring men consulted together what had better be done, as they knew it was impossible to live honestly on such scanty means. I had seen at different times accounts of Trade Societies; I told them of this, and they willingly consented to form a Friendly Society among the labourers, having sufficiently learnt that it would be vain to seek redress either of employers, magistrates or parsons. . . . Shortly after, two delegates from a Trade Society paid us a visit, formed a Friendly Society among the labourers, and gave us directions how to proceed. This was about the latter end of October, 1833. . . .

Nothing particular occurred from this time to the 21st of February, 1834, when placards were posted up . . . cautions from the magistrates, threatening to punish with seven years transportation any man who should join the Union. This was the first time that I had heard of any law being in existence to forbid such societies. . . . February 24th . . . Mr. James Brine, constable of the parish, met me and said, "I have a warrant for you, from the magistrates. . . ." Accordingly I and my companions walked in company with the constable to Dorchester, about seven miles distant . . . and we were instantly sent to prison. As soon as we got within the prison doors, our clothes were stripped off . . . our heads shorn. . . . Mr. Young, an attorney employed on our behalf . . . inquired if I would promise the magistrate to have no more to do with the union if they would let me go home to my wife and family . . . "give them information concerning the Union, who else belongs to it. . . ."

"Do you mean to say I am to betray my companions? . . . No I would rather undergo punishment."

The same day we were sent to the high jail. . . . In this situation, the chaplain of the prison paid us a visit . . . after upbraiding and taunting us with being discontented and idle, and wishing to ruin our masters, he proceeded to tell us that we were better off than our masters and that government had made use of every possible means . . . to make all comfortable. . . .

As to the trial, I need not mention but little . . . suffice it to say, the most unfair and unjust means were resorted to in order to frame an indictment against us; the Grand Jury appeared to ransack heaven and earth to get some clue against us, but in vain . . . and when nothing whatever could be raked together, the unjust and cruel judge Williams ordered us to be tried for mutiny and conspiracy under an act . . . for the suppression of mutiny amongst the mariners and seamen. . . . The greater part of the evidence against us . . . was put into the mouths of the witnesses by the judge . . . among other things he told them . . . if they should not find us guilty, he was certain they would forfeit the opinion of the grand jury . . . landowners. . . .

Two days after this we were again placed at the bar to receive sentence, when the judge told us that not for anything we had done, or, as he could prove, we intended to do, but for an example to others, he considered it his duty to pass the sentence of seven years' transportation. . . .

b) THE LONDON DEMONSTRATION

Last Monday was a day in Britain's history which long will be remembered; for labour put its hat upon its

head and walked towards the Throne. . . . Its heavy
tread made Statesmen tremble . . . and far and near an
anxious people awaited the result. . . . Group after
group of Labour's children marched onward to the
gay green field . . . rank after rank in thick succession
. . . a band of simple men they were devoted to a
just and powerful purpose. No brawls disturbed the
great assembly. No force was needed to provoke good
discipline. . . .

Scarcely had day dawned . . . before the metropolis,
in all its principal streets, began to present the busy note
of preparation for the impending great meeting in Copen-
hagen-fields, and procession thence to Westminster, as an
escort to the five deputies appointed to convey the
petition on behalf of the Dorchester labourers . . . to the
King. Persons were to be seen with the appointed dis-
tinguishing ribbon of the Unions in almost every street
as early as six o'clock this morning. . . . At seven o'clock
. . . . A procession eight abreast . . . extended from
Leather-lane down Holborn-Hill, as far as the eye could
command . . . bodies closely compacted, and walking in
strict order, were to be seen crossing the fields on all
points towards the general point of conveyancing . . . the
new Caledonian Asylum. . . . The confluence at the
Caledonian Asylum . . . was . . . immense. . . . A similar
large body was to be seen advancing along the road over
the Maiden-lane bridge . . . banners were planted in the
open space in front of Copenhagen-house . . . to admit of
the various bodies . . . each ranging himself under his
appropriate trade banner. . . .

The whole of the Unions are now on the ground, and
have been arranged in most admirable order. The
banners, inscribed with the name of the respective trades,
have been planted twenty feet apart, on parallel lines on
either side of the roadway. . . . In compact bodies, six
abreast, the trades are placed in a right line stretching
along the field . . . everything at present wears the dress
of a gay spring holiday. The men appear to be all sober.
None but Unionists are allowed to join the ranks . . .

a body of about 3,000 weavers from Spitalfields have arrived. . . .

The car has just been brought out. . . . The petition is on a wooden roller. . . . It is well engrossed on parchment and is about two feet broad and three in length. . . .

Within a minute after the car had been brought out, the signal rocket was fired off . . . and arrangements . . . commenced for putting the mighty mass of people assembled into orderly motion. . . .

The procession having commenced to move at half-past nine o'clock, proceeded by the prescribed route, accompanied the whole way by vast multitudes. The Rev. Dr. Wade, in canonicals, as Chaplain to the Council, walked with Mr. Owen, immediately after the petition. . . .

The petition has just been taken into the Home Office, and the procession now extends from Parliament Street to the place from which it set out. . . .

23. TRADES UNIONS AND THE STATE, 1834

From the *Pioneer*, May 31st, 1834. The reference to "the Guardian" is to *The Poor Man's Guardian* (No. 69).

. . . UNIVERSAL Suffrage is the fundamental principle of a Trades' Union, where every brother is understood to have a voice in the management of the common affairs of the trade. But it is a Universal Suffrage which begins with the elements of government and not, like the democratic principle of the Guardian and his friends, with the universal business of political legislation. . . .

We are at present so miserably divided . . . upon some of the most simple and elementary principles of politics and morality that it is utterly impossible that unanimity of council in general politics could be secured by an appeal to the voice of the people. . . . Their eyes . . . are so short-sighted that they look only to partial release,—the diminution of taxation, separation of Church and State, revision of pension list and such other milk-and-water favours; and when they have received their boon, pray where are they? Is the power of private capital and monopoly in any wise impaired? Is the commercial system paralysed? And finally, have the working classes obtained any practical knowledge by scrutinising the measures of government? . . . No, none of these objects is gained. There is only one way of gaining them, and that is by a general association of the people for the purpose of initiating themselves into the practice of conducting those affairs in which they have some experience.

The Unions are of all the other means the only mode by which universal suffrage can be safely obtained, because it is obtained by practice . . . by serving an apprenticeship . . . the growing power and growing intelligence of a Trades union . . . will draw into its vortex all the commercial interests of the country, and, in so doing, it will become, by its own self-acquired importance, a most influential, we might almost say dictatorial part of the body politic.

When this happens we have gained all that we want; we have gained universal suffrage, for if every member of the Union be a constituent, and the Union itself become a vital member of the State, it instantly erects itself into a House of Trades which must supply the place of the present House of Commons, and direct the commercial affairs of the country, according to the will of the trades which compose the associations of industry. This is the ascendancy scale by which we arrive to universal suffrage. It will begin in our lodges, extend to our general union, embrace the management of trade, and finally swallow up the whole political power.

24. GLASGOW COTTON SPINNERS' STRIKE,
1837

> The strike and trial described below made a deep impression on the country. The prisoners, charged with illegal conspiracy and murder, were acquitted of the latter, but convicted of the former offence. The whole incident was used by the authorities to blacken trade unionism, but it evoked expressions of working-class solidarity far outside Glasgow. Extracts are from the *Report of the Trial of Thomas Hunter, Peter Hackett, Richard McNeil, James Gibb and William McLean*, by A. Swinton, 1838: *a*) App. p. xxvi; *b*) pp. 185–7; *c*) pp. 295–300.

a) RESOLUTION OF THE OPERATIVE COTTON SPINNERS, MAY, 1837

A GENERAL meeting of the Operative Cotton Spinners of Glasgow was held on 23rd May current, at which it was . . . unanimously resolved *First*, That the meeting being informed that the public have been led to believe, that the disturbances at the factories under strike have been instigated, or promoted by the members of the union, the meeting feel themselves called upon to disabuse the public mind, and to disavow, as they now do, all connection, directly or indirectly, with such disturbance.

Second, That although the meeting cannot subscribe to the doctrine which some of the authorities have laid down as law, viz, that a man may be punished for walking near the works under strike, although he does not, by word or deed, molest any person; yet in order to testify to the world, that the members of the Union are not aiders or abettors in the annoyance said to be given to the new hands, the members of the Union resolve not only to abstain from walking, unnecessarily, near the works, but to use their influence to dissuade others from being guilty of any offence, which the authorities may construe into intimidation or molestation.

I am a cotton spinner, and a member of the association and have been so for rather better than five years. I was admitted at Glasgow in William Smith's Black Boy Tavern. No oath *whatsomever* was administered to me on my admission. I am quite sure of that. No obligation *whatsomever* to observe secrecy was administered or taken; and I never heard of such a thing as any obligation, or undertaking to do acts of violence of any kind to person or property. . . . The general purpose of the association was to support a just and lawful strike, when the masters reduced the wages, and to keep up the rate of wages, if we thought it just and lawful. I recollect the strike in April last quite well. I was working at Mr. Hussey's then. I was a delegate from that mill. . . . The duty of the delegate is to take the sense of the shop to a meeting of delegates, and also to vote. . . .

. . . I was appointed a delegate about a fortnight or three weeks after the strike. . . . I went to a delegate meeting at Mr. Smith's. . . . There was not at that meeting any proposal made by any body to elect a secret . . . committee . . . nor any committee . . . the purpose of which was to control or superintend acts of violence of any kind. . . . I attended all the meetings of delegates in June and I never heard of the proposal of any such committee *whatsomever* at any of them. . . . I have heard of a guard committee. It was for the purpose of seeing if any of our hands were going in and deceiving us, by receiving aliment from our funds, . . . they were to do no more to the new hands, but to offer them the same aliment we were getting, and to do nothing more. The guards were to persuade them by fair means. . . . I have acted as guard myself during the last strike. . . . I went to see if any new hands were going in, and any of our hands, if I knew them, that I might report them, and they would receive no more aliment. . . . A man did not remain a member if he worked after a strike. Such men generally went by the name of nobs. . . . I have heard that nobs were molested, but the guards acted against the law if they used violence or foul language . . . I have heard guards get a reprimand for . . . using violence . . . I heard of the guards being taken off in May . . . because of some disturbances and some persons having been taken up. . . .

c) SPEECH BY COUNSEL FOR THE DEFENCE

. . . The statement made against them is in substance this:—The prosecutor says, that an association was formed in Glasgow . . . to keep up the rate of wages,—that it bound the members by secret oaths,—that, occasionally it directed the members to strike; and that they did strike and that during these strikes . . . they . . . conspired to do certain deeds of violence to forward their object of raising the rate of wages. . . . It is in reference to the things done . . . at and after the strike of 1837—that you are trying the prisoners. The things . . . consist of various acts of violence . . . I am not going to question the fact, that, at Oakbank Factory, guards were placed . . . that Farmer and Gordon . . . Gray and Kean . . . were assaulted. . . . I am not going to dispute that certain things, apparently combustibles, were thrown into Hussey's Mill. . . . Finally I do not dispute that John Smith was cruelly murdered . . . but the defence I make is this, that the persons for whom I attend you, had nothing to do with the perpetration of any of these offences . . . the prosecutor has signally failed in proving that any secret committee existed in 1837. . . . There was a guard committee. . . . That the prisoners were not members of the guard committee is proved. . . .

Another class of illegal acts charged against the Association, is the writing and sending of threatening letters . . . there is not a particle of evidence to connect the prisoners . . . with the sending of threatening letters. . . . So also in regard to the attempts at fire-raising . . . there is nothing to connect the association, or any member of it, with the attempts at fire-raising.

All then that you have against the prisoners is this.

They were members of an association having a lawful object. In April 1837, that Association struck work. . . . The association had a committee of supply, the objects of which were perfectly lawful and of that committee the prisoners were members and office bearers—none of these things are the crimes charged. The prisoners are being charged with . . . illegal Conspiracy; and of certain specific acts of violence done under that conspiracy . . . that the association appointed a secret committee and that this committee hired men to carry these things into execution. I say that there is no trace of all this. . . .

Part Three

IN THE VILLAGE

25. PAUPERS, 1816

From *Cobbett's Weekly Political Register*, May 18th, 1816.

JUST after Easter Tuesday, the officers of the several Parishes hold a meeting, at which, by the way of lottery, they distributed amongst the most able parishioners, *young paupers* to be kept by the said parishioners and brought up by them in their own houses, or at any rate, maintained by them, clothed, fed, lodged, and doctored at their own particular expense, until they grew up to be men, or women.

Luckily I have just had drawn for me in this lottery: a girl about 10 or 12 years of age . . . if I had had all my share of paupers *quartered* upon me as this girl was, I should have had about twenty eight of all ages. . . .

. . . It is from facts like these that we are enabled to judge the real state of the nation. The coaches and chariots and landaus that rattle through the squares and streets of London . . . the loads of pearls and diamonds that shine at the court . . . all these may exist, and the nation be plunged into the deepest of misery and degradation. . . .

What I complain of, is a state of things, which takes so large a part of the children from their natural guardians . . . and throws them upon the mercy of those who are utter strangers to them. . . .

26. AGRICULTURAL LABOURERS' RISINGS, 1830–1

The "last labourers' revolt," the movement of 1830–1 in the south, was the aftermath of the enclosures and of the destruction of home industries, combined with the impact on food prices of the Corn Laws, the introduction of threshing machines, and a severe economic crisis. Local traditions of its brutal suppression lived on into the twentieth century. Nine men and boys were hanged, 457 transported as convicts and about 400 imprisoned. Despite their sinister symbol, "Swing," the labourers killed nobody. Extracts are from *Cobbett's Weekly Political Register*: *a*) November 13th, *b*) November 20th, *c*) December 4th, 1830, *d*) *ibid*.

a) FIRES

GREAT alarm prevails at Hounslow, Bedfont, Northide, Lumpton and Heston amongst the farmers and agriculturists, for the safety of their property, in consequence of the work of incendiaries having commenced in the neighbourhoods above named; and threatening letters have been sent to . . . farmers and gentlemen who have estates upon which they have for some time used machinery instead of hand labour. . . . The threatening epistles are signed, as they are in Kent, by the name of "Swing," and they are to the same purport. About a fortnight since, one of them was sent to Mr. Sherwin, at Bedfont, declaring that unless he immediately dispensed with his threshing machines his barns should be razed to the ground. Mr. Sherwin took no notice of the threat . . . his two barns, several outhouses, and stabling were discovered to be on fire. . . . The incendiaries previous to firing the stables had removed the horses. . . .

b) LABOURERS' WAR, SUSSEX

On Saturday, property to a considerable amount was destroyed by fire on a farm at Dallington, situated between Battle and Heathfield. The risings of the peasantry have continued to increase. On Thursday they collected in considerable numbers at Mayfield; and going from farm to farm they pressed all they came near into their ranks.

Remonstrance and entreaty were vain; farmers, trades-people and labourers, all were obliged to congregate and accompany the multitude. On this occasion they visited the Rev. Mr. Kirby, whose tithes, for a portion of that parish, amounted to £1,200 or £1,400 a year. They demanded that he should immediately reduce them to £400 and that the rest should be remitted to the farmers, to enable them to allow their labourers 2/3 and 2/6 a day, to which Mr. Kirby consented. They then went to the house of Thomset, bailiff to Lord Carrington, where a Mr. Read was lodging. Mr. Read hires of his Lordship the other portion of his tithes amounting to £700 a year. They demanded of this gentleman that he should forth-with saddle and bridle his horse; which being done they ordered him to mount, which he also complied with. Two men then took the bridle, one on each side, and accom-panied with drum and fife, and followed by hundreds of the populace he was escorted out of the parish . . . they bade him good speed, demanding that he *might never again be seen in the parish* under severe pains and penalties. Mr. Read expressed his readiness to follow their instructions. . . .

At Pulborough . . . a meeting of the farmers and other inhabitants of this Parish was held. . . . As soon as a con-siderable number of farmers and others were assembled . . . a deputation of four, from the people assembled out-side the door, entered the room and said in a tone that indicated stronger feeling, "Have you, gentlemen, a mind to give us 2/- a day. We are come here tonight for an answer and an answer we must have before we go. We have been starving on potatoes long enough. . . ." The demand was agreed to. Some of the men said, "We know what they have done in Kent, but we don't wish to do the same if we can help it."

c) HUMBLE PETITION OF THE FARMERS OF THE PARISH OF
WOOD DALLING IN THE COUNTY OF NORFOLK

Sheweth,
    That your petitioners are on the verge of absolutely being ruined; that the destruction of their property is
H

hourly menaced, unless they pay wages which must reduce them to beggary; that the burdens of tithes and taxes have compelled them to reduce the wages of their labourers so much, that they and their families have been reduced to a state of perfect wretchedness, that they have hitherto borne their sufferings with deep complaint, but without violence; but that they now will endure their sufferings no longer; that they have risen to demand that which we know to be their right, but which we are, on account of the tithes and taxes, unable to give without ruin to ourselves . . . on the one side, the labourers have the power of destroying our property . . . on the other side, the clergy and the tax gatherer take from us the means of paying due wages, so as to save ourselves from destructive fires . . . we implore your Honourable House . . . to repeal and abolish the taxes on the necessaries of life, particularly on malt and hops, and reduce the tithes, leaving only a competence for the clergy who actually do the duties of the Church. . . .

d) WILLIAM COBBETT TO THE EDITOR OF *LA REVOLUTION*, PARIS, LONDON, DECEMBER 1ST, 1830

Sir,

The working people in almost all, if not all of the counties of England, are in a state of commotion; all across the South, from Kent to Cornwall, and from Sussex to Lincolnshire, the commotion extends. It began by the labourers in Kent entering the buildings of the great farmers, and breaking their thrashing machines; . . . The labourers of England see, at any rate, that the thrashing machines rob them of the wages they ought to receive. They therefore began by demolishing these machines. This was a *crime*; the magistrates and jailors were ready with punishments; soldiers, well fed and well clothed out of the taxes, were ready to shoot or cut down the offenders. Unable to resist these united forces, the labourers resorted to the use of *fire*, secretly put to the barns and stacks of those who had the machines, or whom they deemed the causes of their poverty and misery. The mischief and the alarm they have caused by this means go beyond all calculation. They go in bands of from 100 to 1,000 men, and summon the farmers to come forth, and then they demand that they shall agree to pay them such wages as they think right. . . .

The farmers, in their defence, say they cannot pay the wages that are demanded, because they have so much to pay in rent and taxes and in tithes. The labourers have, therefore, in many instances gone to the parsons, and *compelled them to reduce their tithes*. . . . These proceedings would have been put to an end had it not been for the FIRES. The military forces . . . would have subdued these half-starved machine breakers; but for the FIRES! No power on earth could have prevented them if the millions of labourers resolved to resort to them. . . .

27. BOYHOOD AND YOUTH OF JOSEPH ARCH, 1835–42

From *Joseph Arch: The Story of His Life, Told by Himself*, 1898, pp. 5–38. In 1872 Joseph Arch led the first large-scale strike of agricultural labourers since the "revolt" of 1830–1 (No. 26). See Vol. II of this series.

My father was a sober, industrious, agricultural labourer, steady as old Time, a plodding man, and a good all-round worker, who could turn his hand to anything, like his father before him.

He was quiet and peaceable by nature. . . . But he could be independent and show a stiff back if it came to a question of principle; and he had no mind to bend his neck to squire or parson for the sake of their doles, when they wanted him to do what he thought was wrong. . . . He showed that, to his cost and ours, when he refused to sign a petition in favour of the Corn Laws.

This petition was properly hall-marked by the local magnates; they sanctioned it, and they put their signatures to it; but my father was a staunch Repealer, and would have nothing to do with such a document. He was made to pay, and we with him, for his honest adherence to principle. Because he dared to speak out and assert what he believed to be right and true; because he, a poor labourer, stood firm for Repeal; because he held on to his opinion he was a marked man for the rest of his life. . . .

It was 1835. . . . Because my father had refused to sign for "a small loaf and a dear one," he could not get any work whatever for eighteen weeks. He tried hard to get a job, but it was useless; he was a marked man, and we should have starved if my mother had not kept us all by her laundry work.

It was a terrible winter. . . . The scenes I witnessed then made an indelible impression on my mind. I have often told the Tories, "You caused the iron to enter into my soul very young, and you will never draw it out. It will remain there till I die."

There was corn enough for everybody—that was the hard, cruel part of it—but those who owned it would not sell it out when it was so sorely needed. They kept it back, they locked it up; and all the time the folk were crying out in their extremity for bread,—crying out to men who hardened their hearts and turned deaf ears to the hungry cries of their starving fellow-creatures. To make as much money as they could, by letting corn rise to famine prices, was all the owners of it cared about. "Make money at any price" was their motto. They belonged to the class of men who always try to turn to their own profit the miseries, the misfortunes, and the helplessness of their poorer neighbours. They grew fat at the expense of their fellows. Those who ruled in high places, and had the making of the laws in their hands, were chiefly rich landowners and successful traders, and instead of trying to raise the people, create a higher standard of comfort and well-being, and better their general condition, they did their best—or worst—to keep them in a state of poverty and serfdom, of dependence and wretchedness. Those who owned and held the land believed, and acted up to their belief as far as they were able, that the land belonged to the rich man only, that the poor man had no part nor lot in it, and had no sort of claim on society.

If a poor man dared to marry and have children, they thought he had no right to claim the necessary food wherewith to keep himself and his family alive. They thought, too, every mother's son of them, that, when a labourer could no longer work, he had lost the right to live. Work was all they wanted from him; he was to work and hold his tongue, year in and year out, early and late, and if he could not work, why, what was the use of him? It was what he was made for, to labour and toil for his betters, without complaint, on a starvation wage. When no more work could be squeezed out of him he was no better than a cumberer of other folk's ground, and the proper place for such as he was the churchyard, where he would be sure to lie quiet under a few feet of earth, and want neither food nor wages any more. A quick death and a cheap burying—that was the motto of those extortioners for the poor man past work.

Being a little chap at the time, I did not realise all that—it was not likely—but I remembered what I saw with my own eyes and heard with my own ears. About the time of the Repeal things had got so bad they could hardly be worse. The food we could get was of very poor quality, and there was far too little of it. Meat was rarely, if ever, to be seen on the labourer's table; the price was too high for his pocket,—a big pocket it was, but with very little in it; next to nothing most days, and sometimes nothing at all! In many a household even a morsel of bacon was considered a luxury. Flour was so dear that the cottage loaf was mostly of barley. Tea ran to six and seven shillings a pound, sugar would be eightpence a pound, and the price of other provisions was in proportion. . . .

We labourers had no lack of lords and masters. There were the parson and his wife at the rectory. There was the squire, with his hand of iron overshadowing us all. There was no velvet glove on that hard hand, as many a poor man found to his hurt. He brought it down on my father because he would not sign for a small loaf and a dear one; and if it had not been for my mother, that hand would have crushed the life right out of him. At the sight of the squire the people trembled. He lorded it right feudally over his tenants, the farmers; the farmers in their turn tyrannised over the labourers; the labourers were no better than toads under a harrow. Most of the farmers were oppressors of the poor; they put on the iron wage-screw, and screwed the labourers' wages down, down below living point; they stretched him on the rack of life-long, abject poverty. . . .

The labourer who had a big family was blamed for it, and treated accordingly. I know for a fact that, when some of the men had a large number of children and were unable to keep them, the parish authorities used to take several of them away and put them in the work-house. It was a disgraceful state of things, from which there seemed no loophole of escape. Parents pauperised because of their children, children pauperised from their youth up because their fathers, however willing, were not able to feed and clothe them. . . .

I went on working in the stables until I was about sixteen, and then I started mowing for the same banker. He used to pay me eighteenpence a day for what he would have had to pay another man half-a-crown. I knew this well enough, and the thought of the extra shilling which should have been in my pocket and was not, rankled and continued to rankle, though I kept pretty quiet about it at the time. In the succeeding summer I joined a gang of mowers, all in the banker's employ; we worked from five o'clock until seven, but not a farthing's increase on my wage did I get, though I was now as expert with the scythe as the best mower among them. I felt the injustice of this treatment more and more keenly, but I dared not speak out,—the time for THAT had not come, and I could not risk the loss of my earn-ings, for my father was in receipt of only eight shillings a week just then. We had to practise the strictest economy in order to keep the wolf of hunger at bay.

Part Four

THE STRUGGLE FOR POLITICAL AND
SOCIAL RIGHTS, 1830–40

28. THE NATIONAL UNION OF WORKING CLASSES, 1831

Extracts below are from *The Life and Struggles of William Lovett*, 1876: *a*) p. 68; *b*) p. 72. Lovett (1800–77), a Cornish ropemaker who became a London cabinet-maker, was among the chief political leaders of the London artisans in the years immediately before and after the Reform Act of 1832 and the outstanding Chartist advocate of "moral force." After his imprisonment 1839–40 he devoted himself to education. See also Nos. 29, 31, 33, 36, 37, 40, 66, 69.

Extract *b*) should be studied with No. 33. Both reflect the outlook of radical artisans, untouched by the factory system, who were continuing older traditions on a more independent working-class basis. The Declaration was drafted by Lovett and James Watson (No. 68). Men of the N.U.W.C. formed the extreme Left wing in the London radical movement before the Reform Act (No. 30); they were nicknamed the Rotundists because they met in the Rotunda near Blackfriars Bridge, leased by Richard Carlile (No. 67).

a) A NEW ASSOCIATION

IN 1831, I joined a new Association, composed chiefly of working men, entitled "The National Union of the Working Classes and Others," its chief objects being "the Protection of Working Men; the Free Disposal of the Produce of Labour; an Effectual Reform of the Commons' House of Parliament; the Repeal of all Bad Laws; the Enactment of a Wise and Comprehensive Code of Laws; and to collect and organize a peaceful expression of public opinion." This Association was organized somewhat on the plan of the Methodist Connexion. *Class-leaders* were appointed at public meetings of the members in the proportion of one for about every thirty or forty members; the Class-leaders mostly meeting with their classes weekly at their own houses. At those meetings political subjects were discussed, and articles from the newspapers and portions of standard political works read and commented on. Branches of the Union were established in various parts of the Metropolis. Public meetings were held weekly in various districts, and speakers appointed to attend them. A great number of similar associations were also organized in different parts of the country. Those associations were greatly efficient in aiding our agitation in favour of a Cheap and Unrestricted Press; in extending public opinion in favour of the Suffrage of the Millions; and in calling forth the condemnation of the people against various unjust and tyrannical acts of the authorities of the day. . . .

b) DECLARATION OF THE N.U.W.C., 1831

"Labour is the Source of Wealth . . ."
"That Commonwealth is best ordered when the citizens are neither too rich nor too poor."—THALES.

At this moment of great public excitement, it is alike the interest as well as the duty of every working man to declare publicly his political sentiments . . . in accordance with which we, the working classes of London, declare:—

"1.—All property (honestly acquired) to be sacred and inviolable.

"2.—That all men are born equally free, and have certain natural and inalienable rights.

"3.—That all governments ought to be founded on those rights; and all laws instituted for the *common benefit in* the protection and security of *all the people*: and not for the particular emolument or advantage of any single man, family, or set of men.

"4.—That all hereditary distinctions of birth are unnatural, and opposed to the equal rights of man; and therefore ought to be abolished.

"5.—That every man of the age of twenty-one years, of sound mind, and not tainted by crime, has a right, either by himself or his representative, to a free voice in determining the nature of the laws, the necessity for public contributions, the appropriation of them, their amount, mode of assessment, and duration.

"6.—That in order to secure the unbiassed choice of proper persons for representatives, the mode of voting should be *by ballot*, that intellectual fitness and moral worth, and *not property*, should be the qualifications for representatives, and that the duration of Parliament should be but for *one year*.

"7.—We declare these principles to be essential to our protection as working men—and the only sure guarantees for the securing to us the proceeds of our labour. . . ."

29. THE CHOLERA PLAGUE: A DEMONSTRATION, 1832

Cholera broke out frequently between 1830 and 1850, due to the absence of public health regulations and the general squalor of the living conditions of the people. This extract from Lovett, *op. cit.*, p. 78, illustrates the rationalistic outlook of the N.U.W.C. (See Nos. 28, 67–73.)

In March, 1832, the Government . . . ordained a general fast to be observed throughout the kingdom, for beseeching God to remove the cholera from among us. Now, most of the members of our union had seen enough in Spitalfields and other districts at that period to convince us that the ravages made by that dreadful disease were chiefly to be attributed to the want and wretchedness that prevailed there; . . . We believed also that the causes that matured and extended that disease were greatly within the power of Government to remove; and, therefore, saw in this proposed fast an attempt on the part of rulers to father their own iniquitous neglect upon the Almighty. We saw also that the bigots who originated and promoted the solemn mockery, were first and foremost among those whose injustice, oppression, and gross neglect had occasioned so much ignorance, poverty, and misery in the country, and consequently their concomitants of filth and disease. We resolved, therefore, from the first, that we would not comply with this piece of hypocrisy, but that we would enter into a subscription to provide the members of our union with *a good dinner on that day*; those who could afford it to provide for those who could not. This we conceived would be a better religious observance of the day than if we had selfishly feasted (as we knew many would) on salt fish with egg sauce, and other delicacies. . . .

We understood from our legal advisor that there was no law to prevent us from forming a peaceable procession through the streets at any time, provided we had no flags, nor banners, nor weapons of defence.

On the morning of the fast day we accordingly assembled in Finsbury Square; the *Morning Chronicle* estimating the numbers of our union to be upwards of twenty thousand, and at least a hundred thousand persons in connection with the object of the procession. We there formed ourselves in order four abreast, Hetherington, Watson and myself being at the head of the procession; our object being merely to take a walk through the Strand, Piccadilly and Hyde Park, and to return to our respective classes to dine, by way of Oxford Street and Holborn. But this route we were not allowed to take . . . our progress through the Strand was obstructed by the new police drawn across Temple Bar armed with staves and drawn cutlasses. . . . We . . . turned up Chancery Lane into Holborn. Here again was another body of the police drawn across to prevent us from going up Holborn . . . in Tottenham Court Road the police, coming down Howland Street, threw themselves across our procession. . . . Fearing further disturbance if we went on with the procession we drew up in the North Crescent, and there we, having addressed a few words to the people on the object of the procession, they, by our advice, broke up, and retired to their respective classes to dine. . . .

30. THE REFORM ACT, 1832

Extract *a*) is from a leading article in the *Poor Man's Guardian*, November 5th, 1831; *b*) is from a worker's letter in the same paper, April 14th, 1832. See Introduction, p. 25.

a) WE believe you are, by this time, aware of how little "the Bill" benefits yourselves: but you are taught to imagine that the transfer of the "nomination" of members from wealthy individuals to the general body of £10 householders, or "middle men," will be of great service to you, in as much as the latter will be more inclined to do you justice than the former; and you are, naturally enough, led into this delusion by the liberal opinions which they have hitherto professed, and the principles they have advocated: yes, when they themselves had common cause with you for complaint—when your wrongs were theirs,—when they had no suffrages, they, then, could say that all persons should have equal rights, and, accordingly, could unite with you in obtaining what themselves required as much as you: could they do otherwise? could they then object to your having rights equal to their own? how would a suitor look, asking of his judges that charity which, even while he asks for it, he is himself denying to others? thus, then, they were obliged to allow your rights: but now the situation of affairs is wonderfully altered; their battle, thanks to your assistance, is safely won, they think; their position is changed from that of fellow sufferers and fellow plaintiffs into that of masters and judges; and the question is, whether, to all our experience of nature, it is not more than probable that they will feel anxious to maintain their own superiority over you—whether, having gained, as an exclusive advantage, that which they before only claimed in common with you, they will, without obligation, surrender up your just proportion of it.

b) Of all the Bills, or *plots* (for it is nothing else), that ever was proposed on earth, this is the most deceptive and the most mischievous. This Bill proposes to extend the number of the electors to about five times the present amount. This on the face of the measure appears, at first sight, a most liberal alteration. What! extend the number of voters from 150,000 to 600,000 or 700,000? *Most liberal indeed!!!* But now, when we come to see that the liberality is all on one side, and none on the other—when we come to see that those whose influence is already tenfold too great, are to have that influence tenfold increased, while you whose influence is already tenfold too little, are to have that influence (through the great increase of the other) incalculably diminished, it is the most *illiberal*, the most *tyrannical*, the most *abominable*, the most *infamous*, the most *hellish* measure that ever could or can be proposed. Your number is four-fifths of the whole population. Your influence, therefore, at elections (in addition to your right of being elected yourselves) ought to be four times as great as all the rest of the community. Yet your influence will not be more than *one-twentieth-part* of that which will be exercised by those who live on the fruits of your labour. You will in reality, therefore, from fear and fewness of number, have no influence at all. . . .

31. "JUSTIFIABLE HOMICIDE," 1833

Lovett, *op. cit.*, p. 82. Cold Bath Fields, site of the famous prison, is now Mount Pleasant, King's Cross, London.

In May [1833] the unfortunate Calthorpe Street affair took place. This had its origin in a public meeting called by the Union of the Working Classes on the Calthorpe Estate, Cold-Bath Fields, for taking preparatory steps respecting the calling of a National Convention. The proceedings, however, had no sooner commenced than the police made a furious onslaught upon the assembled multitude, knocking down, indiscriminately, men, women, and children, great numbers of them being very dangerously wounded.

In the affray a policeman, of the name of Robert Cully, lost his life, he being stabbed by a person whom he had struck with his truncheon. On the inquest held on him, the following verdict was returned by the jury: "We find a verdict of Justifiable Homicide on these grounds— That no Riot Act was read, nor any proclamation advising the people to disperse; that the Government did not take proper precautions to prevent the meeting from assembling; and that the conduct of the police was ferocious, brutal, and unprovoked by the people; and we, moreover, express our anxious hope that the Government will in future take better precautions to prevent the recurrence of such disgraceful transactions in the metropolis."

32. THE TRADES UNIONS AND POLITICS,
1833

From a series of articles in the *Poor Man's Guardian*,
December 7th, 14th, 21st, 28th, 1833, contributed by
James Bronterre O'Brien. O'Brien (1805–64), later
known as "the Chartist schoolmaster," was the outstanding
thinker and most effective writer of the Chartist movement.
An Irish lawyer, he devoted his life to the working-class
movement. Among papers which he contributed to or at
some time edited were the *Poor Man's Guardian, London
Mercury, Northern Star, National Reformer, Operative,* and
British Statesman. He died in great poverty. See Introduction,
p. 20.

For other discussions on trade union policy, see Nos. 14,
18, 23.

In viewing the struggle which is now in progress between
labour and *capital,* or between the trades' Unions . . . and
the master manufacturers . . . there is one circumstance
which fills us with astonishment and regret—we mean *the
disposition of the chief leaders of the workmen to disconnect their
cause altogether with politics.* This is the most futile and ill-
judged proceeding that can be conceived. When the
workmen . . . entered into Trade Unions . . . they must
. . . have anticipated resistance from their employers. . . .
In fact they have for some time past threatened counter-
combinations . . . and the threat has been already executed
by the manufacturers of Derby. This fact we learn from
. . . the resolutions adopted . . . at a meeting of the
masters . . . of that borough. . . .

Look here fellow workmen! the masters combining—
the Unionists dismissed from work—the women as well
as the men turned out to starve—the peace of the
town endangered—*the mayor and magistrates taking pre-
cautionary measures—and the Dragoon Guards called in from
Nottingham!* . . . Would this be the case under a system of
universal suffrage? By no means. General suffrage would
place the magistracy and Parliament, and consequently

the disposal of the military and police forces in the hands of the entire body of the people, . . . the present objects of the Trades' Unions can never be attained under the existing Government, and for this reason—because they are incompatible with the present form of society, which it is the design of that Government to maintain . . . but then what necessity is there for the contrivance of these things? or what necessity is there for the existing relations between master and man? These are after all the real questions for the millions to ask, . . . the masters . . . having hitherto resisted . . . all attempts . . . of the working classes to obtain the elective franchise, as if dreading that such event would lead to the overthrow of the present unnatural system. . . . This is our real ground of quarrel with them, and were the Trades' Unions wise in their generation, it would be to them . . . the governing motive of their combinations. . . .

*   *   *   *   *

. . . we are convinced that without a share in the Government the Trades Unions will effect no *permanent* good for themselves. . . . Let us not be misunderstood, however. So far as they have gone, we perfectly approve their proceedings. They have combined for objects of real practical utility . . . we hail these coalitions as among the most glorious signs of the times. . . . But . . . it is one thing to conclave, and another to effect the objects of the combination. To effect these, something more is required than the mere power of a *strike* or *turn-out*, which is at present the workman's only weapon of self-protection against usury and oppression . . . Universal Suffrage.

*   *   *   *   *

. . . What seek the Trades Unions? *Increase of wages and a diminution of the hours of labour*; that is to say, to work less, and to get more for it. . . . Who does not see that this is to attack "property"? . . . Common sense tells us that the more the producers get, the less is left for the men of profits. . . . But do *we* find fault with this? Far from it! . . . To attack "property" is . . . to attack robbery

. . . how are we to attack him in the safest and most expeditious manner? . . . we cannot attack him by *law*, for he holds the "law" in his own hands. . . . In our opinion the Trades Unions have hit upon the best way of striking property on the head, provided only that they add Universal Suffrage to their present avowed objects. . . .

*　*　*　*　*

This . . . would unite two great parties– those who expect everything from the representation of Industry in Parliament, and those who trust only to Trades Unions. . . .

33. THE LONDON WORKING MEN'S ASSOCIATION, 1836

The London Working Men's Association, of which Lovett was the Secretary, was the centre of the workers' movement in London. Prominent Radicals of the old school, such as Daniel O'Connell and Francis Place, were associated from time to time with its activities, but it soon became too class-conscious for them. Prominent members were Henry Hetherington, James Watson, John Cleave, Henry Vincent, Robert Hartwell and Julian Harney; the L.W.M.A. was an advance on the N.U.W.C., which had faded away soon after the Reform Act. It arose from the successful campaign for the "unstamped" press (No. 69).

Clause 8, below, on the definition of "working classes" reflects the confusion of this age of transition. See Introduction, p. 17. Extract from Lovett, *op. cit.*, p. 92.

... THE result of our deliberations ... was the formation of "The London Working Men's Association." It was first formed at No. 14, Tavistock Street, Covent Garden, and shortly after we took premises at No. 6, Upper North Place, Gray's Inn Road. The objects of the Association were the following:

"1. To draw into one bond of *unity* the *intelligent* and *influential* portion of the working classes in town and country.

"2. To seek by every legal means to place all classes of society in possession of their equal political and social rights.

"3. To devise every possible means, and to use every exertion, to remove those cruel laws that prevent the free circulation of thought through the medium of a *cheap and honest press*.

"4. To promote, by all available means, the education of the rising generation, and the extirpation of those systems which tend to future slavery.

"5. To collect every kind of information appertaining to the interests of the working classes in particular and society in general, especially statistics regarding the wages of labour, the habits and condition of the labourer, and all those causes that mainly contribute to the present state of things.

"6. To meet and communicate with each other for the purpose of digesting the information required, and to mature such plans as they believe will conduce in practice to the well-being of the working classes.

"7. To publish their views and sentiments in such form and manner as shall best serve to create a moral, reflecting, yet energetic public opinion; so as eventually to lead to a gradual improvement in the condition of the working classes, without violence or commotion.

"8. To form a library of reference and useful information; to maintain a place where they can associate for mental improvement and where their brethren from the country can meet with kindred minds actuated by one great motive—that of benefiting politically, socially, and morally, the useful classes. Though the persons forming this Association will be at times disposed to co-operate with all those who seek to promote the happiness of the multitude, yet being convinced from experience that the division of interests in the various classes, in the present state of things, is too often destructive of that union of sentiment which is essential to the prosecution of any great object, they have resolved to confine their members as far as practicable to the working classes. But as there are great differences of opinion as to where the line should be drawn which separates the working classes from the other portions of society, they leave to the Members themselves to determine whether the candidate proposed is eligible to become a Member."

34. AGITATION AGAINST THE POOR LAW OF 1834

In extract a) Cobbett reports his arguments on the Third
Reading of the Poor Law Bill in the House of Commons
(*Weekly Political Register*, July 12th, 1834). Extracts b) and
c) are from the *London Mercury* (edited by John Bell and
Bronterre O'Brien), March 12th, 1837. d) *London Dispatch*,
January 7th, 1838, is from a speech at Newcastle by Joseph
Rayner Stephens (1805–79), a Wesleyan minister, who,
though expelled from Church in 1834, continued as a
freelance preacher. The outstanding agitator against the
Poor Law of 1834, he was unsurpassed in the violence with
which he attacked that measure. In this speech he refers to
the provisions of the Law which forced members of the same
family to be separated in the workhouse.

a) COBBETT SPEAKS

. . . THIS is the most important subject that ever was
agitated in this country at this time . . . its provisions
come home to the very means of existence of every working man in the kingdom. Already we hear the angry
voices of the labourers in the fields and along the lanes.
Already their menaces are heard; a dreadful convulsion
I verily believe is at hand, unless the Lords shall *take time*
to reflect on this bill. . . . The REAL OBJECT was, in my
opinion, to reduce the people of England to the state of
the people of Ireland; to make them live upon potatoes,
at best; and to submit to occasional famine, in order that
the landlords may put in their pockets, not only the
amount of the poor rates; but the amount of one-half of
the wages which the labourers now receive . . . the ultimate object is, to grind down the English labourers to
potatoes and seaweed. . . .

I deny the *rightful* power of this House to pass this
bill . . . the right of the necessitous to be relieved by
their wealthier neighbours is a prescriptive right, enjoyed
at all times and in all ages. . . .

. . . Pass this bill and you destroy the constitution as

far as it relates to the necessitous . . . you dissolve the
social compact as far as relates to the working people. . . .

b) PROTEST MEETING: A RESOLUTION

"That this meeting considers the resolution lately agreed
to by the guardians of the Morpeth Union, that deceased
persons receiving parochial relief shall not have the accustomed decencies of a Christian burial, to evince a brutal
and heathenish spirit, and to be a violent outrage upon
the feelings of a Christian community."

c) MEETING OF SPITALFIELDS SILK WEAVERS: A SPEECH

. . . He would mention a case, and it was one in a
1000 similar cases, where a poor and industrious man had
applied for relief. He had been out of employment for
some weeks, . . . when almost reduced to starvation he
went with his children to the parochial authorities . . .
examination was taken and he was told to go before the
magistrate and swear to his parish, but no relief was
given to him. He went as he was ordered to the magistrate, and was then desired to go to the board of guardians
on the following day. He attended and 20 lbs. of oakum
were given him to pick; they also gave him a loaf *on
account*. This man, with the assistance of his children,
picked the oakum in five days, but when he took it home
it was not the day on which he could receive the money
for it. . . . He complained of the miserable condition in
which he was, and that his children were starving, and
they gave him another loaf on account. The following
day he took home the oakum, he received *twenty pence* for
it, from which they *deducted the value of the two loaves*.
Another poor man whose wife had been ailing for 13
months, was treated in the same way, and upon his men-
tioning that his wife was too ill to be of any service to
him in picking the oakum, one of the authorities, said,
"Oh, nonsense, don't talk to us about that—prop her up
in bed with the pillows, and she will pick it well enough

then." To be thus treated for being unfortunate and poor, was revolting to the feelings of an Englishman—it was treatment which Englishmen would not long submit to. . . .

d) JOSEPH RAYNER STEPHENS: A SPEECH

If this most damnable law, which violated all this law of God, was continued, and all means of peaceably putting an end to it had been tried in vain, then, in the words of their banner, "*For children and wife we'll war to the knife.*" If the people who produce all wealth could not be allowed, according to God's Word, to have the kindly fruits of the earth which they had, in obedience to God's Word, raised by the sweat of their brow, then war to the knife with their enemies, who were the enemies of God. If the musket and the pistol, the sword, and the pike were of no avail, let the women take the scissors, the child the pin or needle. If all failed, then the firebrand—aye, the firebrand—the firebrand, I repeat. The palace shall be in flames. I pause, my friends. If the cottage is not permitted to be the abode of man and wife, and if the smiling infant is to be dragged from a father's arms and a mother's bosom, [it is] because these hell-hounds of commissioners have set up the command of their master the devil, against our God.

35. PARLIAMENT: A WORKING-CLASS VIEW,
1837

From the *London Mercury*, February 19th, 1837. By Bronterre
O'Brien.

. . . IT is melancholy to witness the time of Parliament
occupied with such frivolous discussions. Session after
session is wasted in rubbishing motions like those of
Hume, which have no other end in view than to subserve
paltry electioneering or partisanship purposes; while
never, even by accident, is any one measure introduced,
which veritably concerns the nation as a whole, or goes
to remove the miseries under which the masses groan.
It would seem as though both factions had silently conspired to render the unrepresented millions as dead in
public interest, as they are dead in law—by studiously
burking everything that concerns them. Their whole talk
is about trade or revenue, or appointments or privileges,
or matters of the like partial interest, which affect only
the members themselves, or the rich plundering fraction
of the country that elects them. To listen to their
"debates," one would suppose that the whole nation consisted of merchants, lawyers, placemen, and the like; and
that it either contained no industrious class at all, or that
such class was too insignificant to be thought about. The
only notice ever taken of the workpeople is when some
alterations or additions are being made to the criminal
law. They are then objects of almost exclusive interest;
but the interest they inspire is not one of pity or justice,
but of vindictive coercion and proscription. Indeed a
glance at our statute book would convince a foreigner
that our laws reserved all their favours and protection
for the rich, and all their penalties and severities for
the poor.

36. ORIGIN OF THE PEOPLE'S CHARTER, 1837

Lovett, *op. cit.*, p. 102. "Our Association" is The London Working Men's Association (No. 33). The pamphlet referred to is *The Rotten House of Commons*, an exposure of the undemocratic "reformed" Parliament, published by the L.W.M.A.

In February, 1837, our Association convened a public meeting at the Crown and Anchor in the Strand, for the purpose of petitioning Parliament for Universal Suffrage, no Property Qualifications, Annual Parliaments, Equal Representation, the Payment of Members, and Vote by Ballot. The petition submitted for the approval of the meeting embraced most of the facts contained in the pamphlet alluded to, its prayer being a brief outline of a Bill embodying "the six points." In fact, the prayer of that petition formed the nucleus of the far-famed *People's Charter*, which may be said to have had its origin at this meeting. The public meeting was the most crowded and at the same time the most orderly one I ever attended. All our resolutions were unanimously agreed to, and our petition signed by about three thousand persons.

37. CHARTISM: THE FIRST NATIONAL PETITION, 1839

Only five points of the Charter were included in this petition, which bears the stamp of its middle-class authorship in Birmingham (see No. 40), and should be compared with the Petition of 1842 (No. 50). Thomas Attwood, the Birmingham banker, who moved its reception by Parliament on July 12th, 1839, represented the small industrialists who supported the Charter. (See Introduction, p. 25.) The motion was seconded by John Fielden, and defeated by 235 votes to 46. John Fielden (1784–1849), cotton manufacturer of Todmorden, Lancs., was a bitter opponent of the 1834 Poor Law and a keen advocate of the movement for shorter hours. The extract is from Lovett, *op. cit.*, Appendix C.

THAT we, your petitioners, dwell in a land whose merchants are noted for enterprise, whose manufacturers are very skilful, and whose workmen are proverbial for their industry. . . .

For three-and-twenty years we have enjoyed a profound peace.

Yet, with all these elements of national prosperity, and with every disposition and capacity to take advantage of them, we find ourselves overwhelmed with public and private suffering.

We are bowed down under a load of taxes; which, notwithstanding, fall greatly short of the wants of our rulers; our traders are trembling on the verge of bankruptcy; our workmen are starving; capital brings no profit, and labour no remuneration; the home of the artificer is desolate, and the warehouse of the pawnbroker is full; the workhouse is crowded and the manufactory is deserted. . . .

The energies of a mighty kingdom have been wasted in building up the power of selfish and ignorant men, and its resources squandered for their aggrandisement. . . .

It was the fond expectation of the people that a remedy for the greater part, if not for the whole, of their grievances would be found in the Reform Act of 1832.

They were taught to regard that Act as a wise means to a worthy end; as the machinery of an improved legislation, when the will of the masses would be at length potential. They have been bitterly and basely deceived. The fruit which looked so fair to the eye has turned to dust and ashes when gathered.

The Reform Act has effected a transfer of power from one domineering faction to another, and left the people as helpless as before. . . .

We come before your Honourable House to tell you with all humility, that this state of things must not be permitted to continue; that it cannot long continue without very seriously endangering the stability of the throne and the peace of the kingdom; and that if by God's help and all lawful and constitutional appliances, an end can be put to it, we are fully resolved that it shall speedily come to an end.

We tell your Honourable House that the capital of the master must no longer be deprived of its due reward; that the laws which make food dear, and those which by making money scarce, make labour cheap, must be abolished; that taxation must be made to fall on property, not on industry; that the good of the many, as it is the only legitimate end, so must it be the sole study of the Government. . . .

Required as we are, universally, to support and obey the laws, nature and reason entitle us to demand, that in the making of the laws, the universal voice shall be implicitly listened to.

WE DEMAND UNIVERSAL SUFFRAGE.

The suffrage to be exempt from the corruption of the wealthy, and the violence of the powerful, must be secret. . . .

WE DEMAND THE BALLOT.

To public safety as well as public confidence, frequent elections are essential.

WE DEMAND ANNUAL PARLIAMENTS.

With power to choose, and freedom in choosing, the range of our choice must be unrestricted. We are compelled by the existing laws, to take for our representatives, men who are incapable of appreciating our difficulties or who have little sympathy with them; merchants who have retired from trade, and no longer feel its harassings; proprietors of land who are alike ignorant of its evils and their cure; lawyers, by whom the honours of the senate are sought after only as means of obtaining notice in the courts. . . .

We demand that in the future election of members of your Honourable House, the approbation of the constituency shall be the sole qualification; and that to every representative so chosen shall be assigned, out of the public taxes, a fair and adequate remuneration for the time which he is called upon to devote to the public service. . . .

Universal suffrage will, and it alone can, bring true and lasting peace to the nation; we firmly believe that it will also bring prosperity.

38. THE SOCIAL AIMS OF CHARTISM

Extract *a*) is from an article by Bronterre O'Brien in the *Operative*, March 17th, 1839; *b*) is from a speech by J. R. Stephens, *Northern Star*, September 29th, 1838 (quoted from M. Beer: *History of British Socialism* 1920 II, p. 47).

a) UNIVERSAL Suffrage means meat and drink and clothing, good hours, and good beds, and good substantial furniture for every man and woman and child who will do a fair day's work. Universal Suffrage means a complete mastery, by all the people over all the laws and institutions in the country; and with that mastery the power of providing suitable employment for all, as well as of securing to all the full proceeds of their employment. . . . The moment the people obtain a Parliament of their own, the whole of Society will undergo a rigid scrutiny. Every art, every profession, every trade and calling, every description of interest and property, will be scrupulously inquired into . . . what the landlords yield . . . in return for . . . rents . . . what the parsons yield . . . [what] the government yields . . . reasons for unequal distribution of wealth. . . .

b) . . . This question of universal suffrage is a knife and fork question, after all, a bread and cheese question, notwithstanding all that has been said against it; and if any man should ask me what I mean by universal suffrage I should reply: That every working man in the land has the right to have a good coat on his back, a comfortable abode in which to shelter himself and his family, a good dinner upon his table, and no more work than is necessary to keep him in good health, and so much wages for his work as should keep him in plenty and afford him the enjoyment of all the blessings of life, which a reasonable man could desire. . . . Behind universal suffrage I want to see that knowledge in the mind, that principle in the heart, that power in the conscience, that strength in the right arm that would enable the working man to meet his master boldly, upright on his feet, without the mark of the bondman upon his brow, and without the blush of shame and slavery upon his cheek. . . .

39. CHARTISM: MORAL AND PHYSICAL FORCE

The following extracts illustrate the controversy which developed between the advocates of moral and physical force as a means of achieving the Chartist demands and should be read in conjunction with No. 42. Extract *a*), from the *Operative*, December 16th, 1838, gives resolutions passed at a meeting of Scottish Chartists in Edinburgh; *b*) and *c*) are from speeches by Feargus O'Connor at Leicester and St. Pancras, quoted from the *Operative*: *b*) December 2nd, *c*) December 23rd, 1838.

Feargus O'Connor (1794–1855), an Irish landowner in class origin, threw himself into the social agitations in the North with prodigious energy. Proprietor of the *Northern Star*, he became the uncrowned king of the Chartists, a position which he held, in spite of many rivals, till 1851; shortly after, sickness removed him from activity. In his greatest period his appeal was above all to the newly born proletariat. See also Nos. 52, 55, 58, 77.

a) THAT this meeting deem it quite unnecessary to express any opinion, whether or no it be constitutional for the people to have arms, and to use them in their own defence; because they have a full conviction that in the present struggle for liberty, the exercise of moral power is completely adequate to maintain it, in defiance of all opposition.

That this meeting, relying with unshaken confidence on the efficacy of the many moral means the people possess for the achievement of their rights, unequivocally denounce, in the strongest terms any appeals to physical force, any exhortations to purchase arms, being fully persuaded such appeals tend to diminish the vast influence of moral power—to draw the people away from its use—to rouse and keep alive the lowest and worst feelings of their natures, to tempt them—smarting as they are, under a sense of manifold wrongs and sufferings—to make unlawful attacks on persons and property—to disgust and alienate the best friends of human freedom, and to bring

K

disgrace on the sacred cause in which the people are so honourably engaged. . . .

b) A great many blind horses have taken fright because they have seen physical force on one side of the road in practice, and on the other side of the road in theory. Why do you pay taxes? Because there is physical force. You are cutting sticks to fight yourselves with. Blackstone says it is right to take up arms when the laws do not protect you. . . . I have said that if there was to be fighting, I should be found fighting on the side of the people. . . .

c) A party of men have sprung up . . . who speak of moral courage and denounce physical force. . . . I do not look upon moral force with the same eye as the "Philosophical Radicals." They consider it moral force to write a strong article in the newspaper . . . [they] have placed upon their banners a motto of which I highly approve, "Peace Law and Order," that is if peace procure the law, then I am for order; but if peace procure not the law, then I am for disorder. Peace to be valuable must procure that which will give the greatest amount of happiness to the people, but if the peace is to be all on one side, I care not for it; I am for peace being general or not at all.

40. THE FIRST CHARTIST CONVENTION, 1839

From Lovett, *op. cit.*, p. 201. See Note to No. 37.

THE General Convention of the Industrious Classes originated with the Birmingham Political Union, as did also the National Rent Fund, the proposal for a Sacred Month, the plan of Simultaneous Meetings, and the first National Petition. This last document was, I believe, drawn up by the late Mr. R. K. Douglas, then editor of the *Birmingham Journal*, an able and talented writer, and a keen, clear, eloquent speaker; one, in fact, of the most efficient men delegated to the Convention. The delegates to this body were, for the most part, appointed by very large bodies of men. The Birmingham meeting was composed of 200,000, the Manchester meeting of 300,000, that of Glasgow of 150,000, of Newcastle of 70,000, and other towns equally large in proportion to their population. The number of delegates composing the Convention was *fifty-three*, many of them representing several places, with the view to economy. Of this number three were magistrates, six newspaper editors, one clergyman of the Church of England, one Dissenting minister, and two doctors of medicine, the remainder being shopkeepers, tradesmen and journeymen. They held their first meeting at the British Coffee House, Cockspur Street, Charing Cross, on Monday, February 4th, 1839, and subsequently met in the hall of the Honourable and Ancient Lumber Troop, Bolt Court, Fleet Street. On their first assembling the Birmingham delegates proposed me as secretary, and, though the proposition was at first strongly opposed by some of the physical force party, I was eventually elected unanimously.

41. FIRST MANIFESTO OF THE CHARTIST CONVENTION, 1839

This Manifesto was issued in response to what was taken to be a threat of force from the Government. Extract from the *Charter*, February 17th, 1839, the official organ of the Convention, published in London.

MEN of Great Britain and Ireland—the day has arrived! We, the representatives of your wishes and sufferings, have met—assembled from all parts of the country—bound together in a unity of object. . . . In vain . . . have we looked for any indication . . . that the ministry or the legislature has at length begun to appreciate the true situation of the country and the wants of the people. . . . Your demand is for Universal Suffrage . . . a right of which no human power can justly deprive you . . . and which you must regain at any risk—peaceably, if you may, forcibly if you must.

If forced to a resort to it in self-defence, even to that last tribunal we are prepared to appeal rather than continue in bondage, and rather to lay our heads upon the block as free men than to rest them on the pillow as slaves . . . such interference however, depends not upon us; and if the infatuation of those in power prompt them to have recourse to it, so surely as in the exercise of it they dare to trench upon the liberties of Britain, so surely shall they be met with that stern resolve which prompts men either to conquer or die. . . .

In politics as in war the post of honour is the post of danger. That post you have confided to our charge. To us you have entrusted the recovery of all the rights you have lost and the defence of all that remains . . . and as you require from us individual attention to the most arduous duties, so from you we demand prudence of conduct—firmness of language—determination of purpose—and energy of action.

42. THE PEOPLE'S RIGHT TO BEAR ARMS

The following extracts reflect the ardent debates on the right to bear arms, which most Chartists treated as the ancient and inalienable right of a free Englishman, to be exercised in defence of the equally fundamental constitutional rights which the ruling classes had alienated from the people. There is continuous emphasis here, and elsewhere, on the view that violence would first be exercised against the Chartists. *a*) is from an Address of the Convention to the People of Britain, *Operative*, May 12th, 1839; *b*) is a resolution of the Convention, from the *Charter*, July 14th, 1839.
For the reference to Birmingham see No. 43.

a) FELLOW Countrymen,—When you elected us to take charge of the National Petition, you limited our trust to the exercise of functions truly constitutional and legal. . . . Aware of our position, your oppressors are moving heaven and earth to bring us into collision with the enemy. They are pouring spies and traitors into your ranks, in order to seduce the unwary into illegal practices. They then pounce upon their victims, and by brutal and unconstitutional treatment, seek to exasperate the people to MADNESS and rebellion.

They have already succeeded in fomenting disturbances in Wales, and they have seduced a few incautious individuals in Lancashire to practice training and drilling in contravention of the six acts. By these and the like perfidious agencies they hope to excite a premature insurrection, of which they might take advantage to dissolve the Convention, to put down all public meetings for the People's Charter, and to abolish the surviving constitutional rights and safeguards, through which we alone can hope to obtain the salvation of the country without anarchy and bloodshed. Not content with these machinations the tyrants are also seeking to arm the rich against the poor under pretence of protecting life and property, of which the tyrants themselves are the only destroyers. Yes, countrymen, they are actually encouraging a project, of arming the enemies of the country at the expense of the State, whilst at the same time they are hunting out pretexts (having the semblance of legality) for dispossessing the Chartists of their rightful arms. If the public Press tells us truly the Ministers just resigned have been base enough to engage to furnish 200 aristocrats in Monmouth-shire with arms paid for out of the taxes.

Here, fellow countrymen, is an openly avowed scheme which, if we suffer to be carried into execution, must crush forever your rising hopes and liberties. What course, then, do we advise? Our advice is, that YOU RIGIDLY OBEY THE LAW; but at the same time be prepared to make your oppressors likewise obey it. Be upon your guard against spies or madmen, who would urge you to illegal practices, but at the same time bear in mind that you have the same right to arm that your enemies have, and that if you abandon that right, your liberties are gone for ever. ... Parade not your arms at public meetings but keep them bright and ready at home ... at the same time fail not to be prepared with these arms to resist any and every unconstitutional attempt to suppress your peaceable agitations by physical violence.

b) That this Convention has read with feelings of inexpressible indignation, the statements said to have been made last night in the House of Commons, by the Secretary of State for the Home Department, relative to the necessity and propriety of employing the Metropolitan Police Force, in various parts of the country, for the suppression of public meetings of the people, peaceably conducted. And further, the approbatory remarks of the same minister, of the bloody-minded and atrocious assault made upon the people of Birmingham, by a portion of that unconstitutional and obnoxious force. And this Convention is of opinion, that wherever and whenever persons assembled for just and legal purposes, and conducting themselves without riot or tumult, are assailed by the police or others, they are justified upon every principle of law and self-preservation, in meeting force by force, even to the slaying of the persons guilty of such atrocious and ferocious assaults upon their rights and persons.

43. IN THE BULL RING, BIRMINGHAM, 1839

The meeting referred to in 42 *b*) is here described by George Jacob Holyoake (1817–1906), who, though prominent in the later stages of the Chartist Movement, owes his place in history rather to his secularist and co-operative activities. He was proud, too, of his internationalism. His autobiography, from which the quotation below is taken, is of great value. *Sixty Years of an Agitator's Life*, by G. J. Holyoake, 1906, Chapter 17.

THE first insurgent affair of which I was a witness, and if not an actor, a sympathiser, was in the Birmingham Bull Ring. . . . A dozen gentlemen in the town who had sympathy with the just discontent of the people, could have kept the peace with applause. The sapient and contemptuous magistrates sent for one hundred policemen from London. Magistrates oftener break the peace than workmen, as they do in Ireland, as they did at Peterloo in 1819—as Sir Charles Warren and Mr. Matthews, acting on their ideas of public duty, did in Trafalgar Square in 1887. Birmingham would not be kept in order by London police, though they were at least their own countrymen, and the Chartists broke down the iron railings around St. Thomas's Church, and drove the London contingent out of the Bull Ring. . . .

Some frenzied men set fire to houses in revenge. Soldiers were brought out, and a neighbour of mine, who happened to be standing unarmed and looking on at the corner of Edgbaston Street, had his nose chopped off. Soldiers, like policemen, soon know when outrages are expected of them. There was no resistance after the police were driven away. At four o'clock next morning I went with my wife, who wished to see whether Mr. Belcher whose house had been fired, needed aid in his household, as she had great respect for him. Although we alone crossed the Bull Ring, the soldiers rushed at us, and tried to cut me down. I did not like them. Until then I thought the duty of a police-man or soldier was to keep his head, protect the people, and keep the peace except in self-defence. The town was sullen and turbulent and had good reason to be so. . . .

44. TRADE UNIONS AND A GENERAL STRIKE

Resolution of the Chartist Convention, August 5th, 1839, from the *Charter*, August 11th, 1839. A previous decision had been made for a general strike or "sacred month" (No. 17) if the Petition (No. 37) was rejected.

THAT from the evidence which has reached this council from various parts of the country, we are unanimously of opinion, that the people are not prepared to carry out the sacred month, on the 12th of August. The same evidence however, convinces us that the great body of the working people, including most of the trades, may be induced to cease work on the 12th instant, for one, two or three days, in order to devote the whole of that time to solemn processions and meetings, for deliberating on the present awful state of the country, and devising the best means of averting the hideous despotism, with which the industrious orders are menaced by the murderous majority of the upper and middle classes, who prey upon their labour.

We, at the same time, beg to announce to the country that it is the deliberate opinion of this council, that unless the trades of Great Britain shall co-operate as united bodies with their more distressed brethren, in making a grand national moral demonstration on the 12th instant, it will be impossible to save the country from a revolution of blood, which after enormous sacrifices of life and property, will terminate in the utter subjection of the working people to the monied murderers of society. Under these circumstances, we implore all our brother Chartists to abandon the project of a sacred month as being for the present utterly impracticable, and to prepare themselves forthwith to carry into effect the aforesaid constitutional objects on the 12th instant. We also implore the united trades, if they would save the country from convulsion, and themselves and families from ruin, to render their distressed brethren all the aid in their power, on or before the 12th instant, towards realising the great and beneficent object of the holiday. Men of the trades! The salvation of the Empire is in your hands.

45. PLAN FOR A CHARTIST PARLIAMENT, 1839

This speech by Bronterre O'Brien is the briefest statement of the scheme for a Parliament elected by the voteless masses to sit, side by side with the legal, but undemocratic, Parliament as a kind of "dual power." Under the electoral system of the time, a show of hands was first taken at the hustings. If the result were challenged, the Returning Officer normally ordered a poll of qualified voters. The Chartists, though unqualified to vote, usually attended the hustings and voted for their own or, perhaps, one of the "official" candidates: hence O'Brien's scheme. From the *Northern Star*, May 25th, 1839.

. . . AT the next general election we must have Chartists as our representatives, and when they have been elected by a show of hands we must insist on having a formal return made to that effect by the returning officers. We shall thus have a Parliament legally chosen under the Queen's Writ, and we shall then soon show our tyrants the difference between a Parliament nominated by nine or ten millions and one elected by three or four thousand monopolists. The people's Parliament will meet at Birmingham and then it may be necessary that 500,000 of their constituents should proceed thither to protect them in the discharge of their legislative duties. . . .

46. THE NEWPORT RISING, 1839

After the Convention's decision against a general strike (No. 44) many Chartists were arrested for possessing arms, etc. This was the situation in which the Convention dissolved and the plan matured for an insurrection in Wales and possibly elsewhere. On November 4th, 1839, a force of Chartist miners and others marched on Newport, where troops killed 14 and wounded 50. To release Henry Vincent, the Chartist leader, from Monmouth Gaol was one aim of the insurgents.

It is impossible to give a satisfactory picture of the Newport Rising in a few extracts. All that is illustrated here is something of the preliminary organisation, of the part played by the leaders, Frost, Williams, and Jones, and of what were possibly the objectives. The evidence at the magistrates' examination, rather than at the subsequent trial, has been quoted because the statements were made on oath immediately after the rising. Extracts *a*) I, II, III, IV, are from the *Charter*, November 10th, November 17th, 24th, December 1st, 1839; *b*) is from the *Charter*, November 1st, 1839; *c*) is from *Memories*, by W. J. Linton, 1895, p. 43–4. The death sentences on John Frost, Zephania Williams and William Jones were commuted to transportation after strong popular agitation.

a I) EVIDENCE OF MATTHEW WILLIAMS

MATTHEW WILLIAMS was then sworn (the witness was badly wounded in the thigh): I am a quarryman . . . at Argoed. . . . That Sunday evening, after we left the lodge, every one was to go home and have refreshment. . . . I went with the party down to Newbridge. I only took a stick with a great knob on the end of it. We were joined by other large parties, most of them armed with sticks, guns, a great many with pikes, one sword, and stakes. . . . At Newbridge it was said that John Frost was gone ahead and we were to come after him. I saw . . . Frost . . . near Risca. . . . All this was in the dead of the night. We then went on to Newport, several hundred of us . . . when Frost came back . . . he gave orders and put us in the way to march. . . . We came through Tredegar Park;

it was then about daylight. We came from Tredegar Park to the top of Stow-hill. . . . I did not see John Frost then . . . the last time I saw him was opposite the Roman Catholic Chapel, two doors from the Westgate. . . . All this armed party were marching in the middle of the road, down the hill, and he was there. . . . I was behind hundreds. . . . There were guns, and I heard the order given, "Fire, fire," when they cried out, "Let us break the windows." I stepped forward. . . . I was knocked down. . . .

a II) A CHARTIST BOY

A lad, about sixteen years of age, named Charles Groves, was then placed at the bar, charged with being found under suspicious circumstances. The prisoner was Secretary to the Chartist Boys' Society. . . .

Mr. George Oliver . . . I am a printer, residing in . . . Newport and know the prisoner. He worked for me last year as a painter. I have several times conversed with the prisoner at the bar about the Chartists. I spoke to him on account of his leaving my work earlier than I wished him to do. . . . It was after Vincent was taken and committed to Monmouth gaol. We offered to pay him any sum for working overtime. He said he would go to attend the Chartist meetings. . . . He said . . . he knew all about their grievances, and they were determined to have the Charter; if they could not have it one way they would another. When I offered him any sum for working overtime, his answer was "No, not if you would give me £5." . . . He never would stay on the evenings that any Chartist meetings were held. . . .

a III) EVIDENCE OF MORGAN JAMES AND GEORGE HODGE

Morgan James was then sworn. . . .

I am a labourer. . . . I have joined the Chartists. . . . I know a man called Jenkin Morgan of Pill. . . . He called on me on the Sunday before the riot, the 3rd of November. . . . He said he was a captain over 10 men.

He said I was his man and I was to come along with him.
. . . He said that Frost and his men by thousands were
coming down that morning to Stow to attack the soldiers.
He said the Charter would be law before daylight; they
would take the whole town and go through the whole
kingdom. He said Frost and his men were to attack the
soldiers. . . . He told me I should have plenty of ammunition when Frost came down. . . . He said the same
movement was to happen through Ireland and Scotland
and everywhere. . . .

. . . He told us how we were to know one another. He
said if I met anyone on the roads I was to say "Beans,"
and the friends of the Chartists were to say "Well." . . .
He told me Frost would attack the soldiers . . . and if
they beat the soldiers they were to rule in this town themselves. We knew what signal they were to give when they
came to the town. They were to throw crackers up in the
air, and as soon as he saw that, he and his men were to
go on duty, and not before. . . .

George Hodge was then sworn and examined.

I am a collier. . . . I live near the Blackwood. I was at
home on Sunday the 3rd of November. . . . A number of
men from 7 to 10 came to my house. They were armed.
A gun or two and a pike or two. . . . At the Coach and
Horses I saw Mr. Frost. . . . There was a considerable
number of men present. . . . Mr. Frost said Zephania
Williams was to meet them at the Cefu with 5,000 men.
Jones of Pont-y-pool, was to meet them with about 2,000.
. . . Some of the men made the remark of what was the
good of going there without arms? Someone made answer
that there were plenty of guns, bayonets and ammunition
there. . . . I ran up to Frost and said to him, "In the
name of God what are you going to do?" "Are you going
to attack any place?" and he said, "Yes; to attack Newport, and take it." He also said he would blow down the
bridge and stop the Welsh mail from proceeding to
Birmingham. He said the delegates were then to be in
waiting an hour and a half after time, and if the mail did
not arrive by that time, they would attack Birmingham

and from there spread all through the North of England.
. . . I implored him not to take us there. He asked me if
I thought so; and turned away with a great deal of scorn.

a IV) EVIDENCE OF JAMES JONES AND JAMES EMERY

James Jones sworn. . . .
I am a miner. I know Zephania Williams. I was at the
Royal Oak on Sunday, the 3rd of November . . . at half
past three o'clock in the afternoon. I saw Zephania
Williams there. . . . There was a man speaking there. . . .
Zephania Williams interpreted the man's speech into
Welsh. He said bring bread and cheese with us, for we
should want some victuals before we came back. He said
we should hear when we were going to the mountains
what we were going for. He told us to bring something
in our hands but did not tell us what. . . . I went to the
mountain. . . . I saw a good many people there. It was
dark and rained shockingly. The people I saw on the
mountain had sticks and one or two guns. It was so dark
I cannot say what else they had. . . . I saw Zephania
Williams on the train road when we had walked down
a bit. . . . I saw a man talking to Zephania Williams. He
asked him what we were going down for—were we going
to be killed. Zephania Williams said, "I hope there is
no danger in our going down, of being killed. . . ."

James Emery sworn. . . .
I am a cabinet maker residing at Pontypool. . . . On
the Tuesday before the 3rd of November I attended a
Chartist meeting at John Llewellin's, at Pontypool . . .
between nine and ten in the evening I saw the prisoner
with upwards of a dozen men come in. . . . There was
a butcher for chairman that night, . . . the chairman
repeated some part of the speech he had been making
before . . . to the effect that he (the chairman) was sent
as deputy round the hills, to see how the organisation
was proceeding in the association. He said there was a
number organised and armed; that the deputation from
Merthyr said they were prepared; great numbers were

already armed and organised. The chairman asked the parties then present if they were prepared for the worst. ... I saw Jones come in; he ordered the men to turn out and proceed in a body to Newport ... the pikemen first, the men with the guns next, and the rest to follow after with what they could get. ...

b) LETTER OF GEORGE SHELL, KILLED IN THE NEWPORT RISING

Pontypool, Sunday Night, Nov. 4th, 1839.

Dear Parents,—I hope this will find you well, as I am myself at this present. I shall this night be engaged in a glorious struggle for freedom, and should it please God to spare my life, I shall see you soon; but if not grieve not for me, I shall have fell in a noble cause. My tools are at Mr. Cecil's and likewise my clothes. Farewell!

Yours truly,

GEORGE SHELL.

c) DEATH SENTENCES

While they were in prison awaiting their trial, I, then living at Woodford, some eight miles from London, had a visit from Watson to tell me that one of the rebels, who had been put in prison chiefly that he might be used as a witness against Frost, had escaped and was then in London, at Hetherington's. Would I give him refuge and take care of him? Of course I would. So he came, little more than a lad (and a nice lad) and stayed with me until the trial was over. ... When news came that the death sentence of the three men was really to be carried out, and that the gallows was being erected, it was in the little sitting-room behind Watson's shop in the City Road that we copied out a petition for reprieve, to which the subscriptions received in not many hours became so numerous that the Government was feign to send the announcement of a stay in the death-sentence to Hetherington's more prominent place of business in the Strand, to be there exhibited to allay popular excitement. ...

47. A VIEW OF HISTORICAL DEVELOPMENT, 1837

By Bronterre O'Brien, *London Mercury*, May 7th, 1837.

WHAT means a social revolution? I mean by it a radical reform in the relative duties and positions of the different classes of society. Political revolutions seldom go beyond the surface of society. They seldom amount to more than a mere transfer of power from one set of political chiefs to another. At best they only substitute one aristocratic form of government for another, and hence all political revolutions of which history makes mention have left the world pretty much as they found it—not wiser—not happier—not improved in any one essential particular. . . . Even the establishment of our "commonwealth" after the death of Charles I was a mere political revolution. It gave parliamentary privilege a temporary triumph over royal prerogative. It enabled a few thousand landowners to disenthral themselves from the burdens of feudal services, and to throw upon the people at large the expenses of maintaining the government . . . for the millions it did nothing. . . .

The revolution of 1688 . . . did no better for the masses . . . instead of a semi-feudal oligarchy of landowners [it] gave us a mixed mongrel aristocracy of landowners and moneymongers to compose our future parliaments. At all events it did nothing for the millions . . . if we except those precious inheritances—the National Debt and the funding system, of which the revolution of 1688 was the undoubted parent.

The American Revolution of 1775 and the French Revolution of 1789 were on a larger scale and of a more democratic character than any of the preceding ones. Nevertheless they were only political revolutions. The French affair . . . sought at first only the overthrow of certain feudal privileges . . . and to fix certain limits to the King's prerogative. By degrees its original character changed, and as the commercial classes began to take part in it it assumed more of the character of our Whig revolution of 1688. The Constitution of 1791 was for the French Bourgeoisie of that epoch what the "Bill of Rights" was for the English Shopocracy of 1688. It divided the government of France between the moneymongers and the landowners. . . . In France . . . the revolution itself was attacked from within and without by the aristocracies of France and Europe. The middle orders on whose behalf it was made were unable to defend it and the millions *would not* without getting a share of the government for themselves. . . . Hence . . . the Constitution . . . of 1793 . . based on universal suffrage. . . . But the democratic constitution of 1793 was . . . never executed. Had it been . . . the revolution would in all probability have been social. . . . The death of Robespierre was the end of the Republic—with him ended all hopes of a social revolution. . . .

The American Revolution of 1775, is the most perfect revolution of its kind that has hitherto been effected in the world . . . taking the states collectively the franchise is sufficiently extended to entitle the government to be called a Democratic Republic. At all events it is the most perfect government of its kind that has hitherto been known to exist . . . however the American people are fast sinking into poverty and slavery. . . . Various are the assigned causes of this downward progress . . . the genuine cause . . . is . . . BAD PROPERTY INSTITUTIONS . . . which . . . allow property to be dishonestly acquired and dishonestly transmitted . . . 1775 did not change the system of acquiring and transmitting property. It was . . . a mere political revolution. In leaving the institution of property where it found it, it left all the germs of social evil to ripen in the womb of time, and these germs remaining, it was of little consequence what the particular form of government was, or might be. . . .

48. THE ECONOMIC EFFECTS OF CLASS SOCIETY

John Francis Bray (1809–95), an American of Yorkshire parentage, lived in England from 1822 to 1842. He was active in the Labour Movement in the North of England, particularly as an advocate of the Socialist ideas of Robert Owen. The extracts are from *Labour's Wrongs and Labour's Remedy*, 1839 (pp. 33, 36–7, 45, 48–52, 67, 88–9, 109–10), which had an important influence on Chartist thought. They illustrate his theory of "equal exchanges," which Marx criticised in *The Poverty of Philosophy*, 1847.

It is labour *alone which bestows value*. . . . Every man has an undoubted right to all that his honest labour can procure him. When he thus appropriates the *fruits* of his labour, he commits no injustice upon any other human being; for he interferes with no other man's right of doing the same with the products of *his* labour . . . all ideas of superior and inferior—of master and man—may be traced to the neglect of First Principles, and to the consequent rise of inequality of possessions; and such ideas will never be eradicated, nor the institutions founded upon them be subverted, so long as this inequality is maintained. Men have hitherto blindly hoped to remedy the present unnatural state of things . . . by destroying *existing inequality*, and leaving untouched the *cause* of the inequality; but . . . misgovernment is not a cause, but a consequence . . . it is not the creator but the created— *that is the offspring of inequality of possessions*; and . . . inequality of possessions is inseparably connected with our present social system. . . . Not only are greatest advantages, but strict justice also, on the side of a system of equality. . . . Every man is a link, and an indispensable link, in the chain of effects—the beginning of which is but an idea, and the end perhaps, the production of a piece of cloth. Thus, although we may entertain different feelings towards the several parties, it does not follow that one should be better paid for his labour than another.

The inventor will ever receive, in addition to his just pecuniary reward, that which genius only can obtain from us—the tribute of our admiration. . . .

From the very nature of labour and exchange, strict justice not only requires that all exchangers should be *mutually* but that they should likewise be *equally* benefited. Men have only two things which they can exchange with each other, namely, labour and the produce of labour. . . . If a just system of exchanges were acted upon, the value of all articles would be determined by the entire cost of production; and *equal values would always exchange for equal values*. If, for instance, it takes a hatter one day to make a hat, and a shoemaker the same time to make a pair of shoes—supposing the material used by each to be of the same value—and they exchange these articles with each other, they are not only mutually but equally benefited: the advantage derived by either party cannot be a disadvantage to the other, as each has given the same amount of labour and the materials made use of by each were of equal value. But if the hatter should obtain *two* pairs of shoes for *one* hat—time and value of material being as before—the exchange would clearly be an unjust one. The hatter would defraud the shoemaker of one day's labour; and were the former to act thus in all his exchanges, he would receive, for the labour of *half a year* the product of some other person's *whole year*. Therefore the gain of the first would necessarily be a loss to the last.

We have heretofore acted upon no other than this most unjust system of exchanges—the workmen have *given* the capitalist the labour of a whole year, in exchange for the value of only half a year—and from this, and not from the assumed inequality of bodily and mental powers in individuals, has arisen the inequality of wealth and power which at present exists around us. It is an inevitable condition of inequality of exchanges—of buying at one price and selling at another—that capitalists shall continue to be capitalists, and working men be working men —the one a class of tyrants and the other a class of slaves—

to eternity. . . . The whole transaction therefore plainly shows that the capitalists and proprietors do no more than give the working man, for his labour of one week, a part of the wealth which they obtained from him the week before!—which just amounts to giving him *nothing* for *something* . . . it is in fact, in thousands of instances, no other than a barefaced though legalised robbery. . . .

. . . The gain of the employer will never cease to be the loss of the employed—until the exchanges between the parties are equal; and exchanges can never be equal while society is divided into capitalists and producers—the last living upon their labour and the first bloating upon the profit of that labour. It is plain . . . that, establish whatever form of government we will . . . we may talk of morality and brotherly love . . . no reciprocity can exist where there are unequal exchanges. . . . Inequality of exchanges, as being the cause of inequality of possessions, is the secret enemy that devours us. . . . So long as this system of unequal exchanges remains in force, the producers will continue to be almost as poor, as ignorant, and as hardworked as they are at present, even if *every* governmental burthen be . . . abolished. . . . Nothing but a total change of system—an equalising of labour and exchanges—can alter this state of things. . . . The producers have but to make an effort—and by them must every effort for their own redemption be made—and their chains will be snapped asunder for ever. . . .

. . . Where equal exchanges are maintained, the gain of one man cannot be the loss of another; for every exchange is then simply a *transfer*, and not a *sacrifice*, of labour and wealth. Thus, although under a social system based on equal exchanges a parsimonious man may become rich, his wealth will be no more than the accumulated produce of his own labour. He may exchange his wealth, or he may give it to others . . . but a rich man cannot continue wealthy for any length of time after he has ceased to labour. Under equality of exchanges wealth cannot have, as it now has, a procreative and apparently self-generating power, such as replenishes all waste from consumption; for, unless it be renewed by labour, wealth when once consumed is given up for ever. That which is now called profit and interest cannot exist as such in connection with equality of exchanges; for producer and distributor would be alike remunerated, and the sum total of their labour would determine the value of the article created and brought to the hands of the consumer.

The principle of equal exchanges, therefore, must from its very nature ensure universal labour. It will consequently be destructive of that great social ulcer, the maintenance of one class at the expense of another because it will prevent the division of society into classes. . . .

Part Five

INDUSTRIAL AND POLITICAL ACTION,
1840–8

49. THE NATIONAL CHARTER ASSOCIATION,
1840

The reorganisation described here, and subsequent ones, helped to strengthen the movement. One result was the very wide circulation of the National Petition in 1842. R. G. Gammage's *History of the Chartist Movement*, 1854, quoted below, is one of the great documents of Chartism. Gammage, a prominent Chartist, was a Northampton shoemaker who became a doctor. From Gammage, p. 197.

THE last of the Chartist prisoners had not been put upon his trial, before an effort was made to remodel the organisation of the Chartist body ... the first associations formed for the Charter were local, though all converging towards the national object. Many of these bodies had become disorganised; and on Monday, the 20th of July, 1840, a meeting of delegates assembled at Manchester to take the subject into consideration, and to devise a plan for placing the body on a better footing. ... After coming to various resolutions with respect to the wives and families of the incarcerated Chartists, the delegates proceeded to discuss various plans of organisation; and after several days' sitting, it was ultimately resolved to merge all the local bodies into one association, to which they gave the name of the "National Charter Association of Great Britain."

The basis of the association was of course the People's Charter; and it was agreed that none but peaceful and constitutional means should be employed for gaining that object. All persons might be admitted as members on declaring that they agreed with the principles of the association, and taking out a card of membership, to be renewed quarterly, for which they should be charged twopence. Where practicable, the members were to be divided into classes of ten, and a leader appointed to each class by the Executive. The latter was to be composed of seven persons, including a secretary and treasurer, who were to appoint a Council, with a sub-secretary and sub-treasurer to be nominated by the members in each locality. The Executive, as well as the General Council, were to be elected annually—the former by a majority of the members throughout the country. The salary of the general secretary was fixed at the rate of £2 per week, and the other members of the Executive were each to receive a weekly salary of £1 10s. during their sittings.

One-half of the monies collected throughout the country were to be at the disposal of the Executive, who, when practicable, were to act as missionaries, and appoint other missionaries to agitate the various districts in favour of the Charter. It was agreed that at the next general election, the Chartists should, wherever practicable, adopt Mr. O'Brien's plan of putting forward Chartist candidates to advocate their principles, and that the Chartist body should attend all public meetings of a political character in order to make known their views, and, if necessary, move amendments to the objects of those meetings.

50. SECOND CHARTIST PETITION, 1842

The Petition was presented on May 3rd, 1842, by Thomas Duncombe (No. 63), and supported, as in 1839, by John Fielden (No. 37). The debate was the occasion of a famous attack on universal suffrage and democracy by Macaulay. The motion was defeated by 287 votes to 49. For the first Petition see No. 37. Extract from *Hansard, Parliamentary Debates*, 1842, Vol. 62. We have throughout omitted the customary opening of sentences in a petition: "that."

. . . YOUR petitioners instance . . . that your honourable House has not been elected by the people, that the population of Great Britain and Ireland is at present about 26 millions of persons, and yet, out of this number little more than 900,000 have been permitted to vote in the . . . election of representatives to make laws to govern the whole. The existing state of representation is not only extremely limited and unjust, but unequally divided and gives preponderating influence to the landed and moneyed interests to the utter ruin of the small trading and labouring classes. The borough of Guildford with a population of 3,920 returns to parliament as many members as the Tower Hamlets with a population of 300,000; Evesham with a population of 3,998 elects as many representatives as Manchester with a population of 200,000 . . . these being but a few instances of the enormous inequalities existing in what is called the representation of this country. Bribery, intimidation, corruption, perjury, and riot prevail at all parliamentary elections to an extent best understood by the Members of your honourable House. . . .

In England, Ireland, Scotland, and Wales thousands of people are dying from actual want; and your petitioners, while sensible that poverty is the great exciting cause of crime, view with mingled astonishment and alarm the ill provision made for the poor, the aged, and the infirm; and likewise perceive with feelings of indignation, the

determination of your honourable House to continue the
Poor Law in operation, notwithstanding the many proofs
which have been afforded by sad experience of the unconstitutional principle of that Bill, of its unchristian character
and of the cruel and murderous effects produced upon
the wages of working men and the lives of the subjects
of this realm. . . .

Your petitioners would direct the attention of your
honourable House to the great disparity existing between
the wages of the producing millions and the salaries of
those whose comparative usefulness ought to be ques-
tioned, where riches and luxury prevail amongst the
rulers and poverty and starvation amongst the ruled . . .
Your petitioners, with all due respect and loyalty, would
compare the daily income of the Sovereign Majesty with
that of thousands of working men of this nation; and
whilst your petitioners have learned that Her Majesty
receives daily for private use the sum of £164 17s. 10d.,
they have also ascertained that many thousands of
families of the labourers are only in receipt of 3¾d. per
head per day . . . your petitioners have also learned that
His Royal Highness Prince Albert receives each day . . .
£104 2s., while thousands . . . exist on 3d. per head per
day. Your petitioners have also learned with astonishment
that the King of Hanover daily receives £57 10s. whilst
thousands of taxpayers of this empire live upon 2¾d.
per head per day . . . your petitioners have with pain and
regret also learned that the Archbishop of Canterbury is
daily in receipt of £52 10s. per day, whilst thousands of
the poor have to maintain their families upon an income
not exceeding 2d. per day. . . .

Your petitioners know that it is the undoubted constitutional right of the people to meet freely. . . . Your
petitioners complain that the right has unconstitutionally
been infringed, and 500 well-disposed persons have been
arrested, excessive bail demanded, tried by packed juries,
sentenced to imprisonment, and treated as felons of the
worst description. An unconstitutional police is distributed
all over the country, at enormous cost, to prevent the due

exercise of the people's rights. And your petitioners are of opinion that the Poor law Bastilles and the police stations, being co-existent, have originated from the same cause, viz., the increased desire on the part of the irresponsible few to oppress and starve the many. A vast and unconstitutional army is upheld at the public expense for the purpose of repressing public opinion in the three kingdoms and likewise to intimidate the millions in the due exercise of those rights and privileges which ought to belong to them.

Your petitioners complain that the hours of labour, particularly of the factory workers, are protracted beyond the limits of human endurance, and that the wages earned, after unnatural application to toil in heated and unhealthy workshops, are inadequate to sustain the bodily strength and to supply those comforts which are so imperative after an excessive waste of physical energy. Your petitioners also direct the attention of your honourable House to the starvation wages of the agricultural labourer, and view with horror and indignation the paltry income of those whose toil gives being to the staple food of the people. . . .

Your petitioners complain that upwards of nine millions per annum are unjustly abstracted from them to maintain a church establishment . . . and entreat you to contrast their deeds with the conduct of the founder of the Christian religion. . . .

Your petitioners complain of the many grievances borne by the people of Ireland, and contend that they are fully entitled to a repeal of the legislative union. . . .

51. HARNEY'S SPEECH AT THE GRAVE OF SAMUEL HOLBERRY, 1840

Holberry, a young Sheffield Chartist who died while serving a prison sentence, was one of 443 political prisoners sentenced in 1839–40 after the first Chartist agitation (Nos. 35–46). His funeral at Attercliffe was the occasion of a great mass demonstration. On his coffin was inscribed: "Samuel Holberry died a martyr to the cause of democracy. June 21st, 1842; age 27." The extract is from Gammage, *op. cit.*, p. 233. For G. J. Harney see No. 76.

OUR task is not to weep; we must leave tears to women. Our task is to act; to labour with heart and soul for the destruction of the horrible system under which Holberry has perished. His sufferings are over; he is where the "wicked cease from troubling and the weary are at rest." He sleeps well; he is numbered with the patriots who have died martyrs to the cause of liberty before him. His is the bloodless laurel, awarded him by a grateful and admiring people. How different to the wreath which encircles the brow of the princely murderer, and the conquering destroyer! Compared with the honest, virtuous fame of this son of toil, how poor, how contemptible appear the so-called glories that emblazon the name of an Alexander or a Napoleon! Desolated empires, or slaughtered myriads, have saved their names from oblivion; but will not, in a future and a better age, save them from execration; whilst with the Tells and Tylers of the earth, the name of Holberry will be associated, venerated, and adored. Be ours the task to accomplish by one glorious effort the freedom of our country, and thereby prevent for the future the sacrifice of the sons of freedom.

52. THE GENERAL STRIKE OF 1842

Extract *a*) is from *The Life of Thomas Cooper written by Himself*, 1877, Chapters 18–20. Thomas Cooper (1805–92), shoemaker and schoolmaster, Chartist agitator, organiser and poet, was the leader of the "Shakespearean Chartists" of Leicester, and one of the chiefs of the national movement from about 1840 to 1846. While he was in prison (1843–5), he wrote *The Purgatory of Suicides*, his best known poem. *b*) is from *The Lancaster Trials*, published by the *Northern Star*, 1843. This manifesto (issued in August, 1842) was drafted by Dr. McDouall, President of the National Charter Association, and led to the arrest of many Chartist leaders, including Feargus O'Connor, and their subsequent trial at Lancaster. McDouall succeeded, after many adventures, in escaping to France. *c*) is from *The Lancaster Trials*. The Chartists were put on trial for conspiracy, unlawful assembly, forcing people to leave their work and for issuing seditious libels, etc. About half the fifty-nine defendants were acquitted. Feargus O'Connor was found guilty on one out of the nine counts of which all were accused. On appeal, a technical flaw led to the release of the prisoners, among them Richard Pilling.

a) THOMAS COOPER IN HANLEY AND MANCHESTER

I was lodging [in Hanley] at honest and devoted Jeremiah Yates'; but often went across the road to the George and Dragon, an inn to which a large room was attached, in which Chartist meetings were usually held. When I reached the inn that night, the Chartist Committee told me they had received instruction from the Chartist Committee in Manchester to bring out the people from labour, and to persuade them to work no more till the Charter became law. . . .

"The Plug Plot," of 1842, as it is still called in Lancashire, began in reductions of wages by the Anti-Corn-Law manufacturers, who did not conceal their purpose of driving the people to desperation, in order to paralyse the Government. The people advanced at last, to a wild general strike, and drew the plugs so as to stop the works at the mills, and thus render labour impossible. Some wanted the men who spoke at the meetings held at the beginning of the strike to propose resolutions in favour of Corn Law Repeal; but they refused. The first meeting where the resolution was passed, "that all labour should cease until the People's Charter became the law of the land," was held on the 7th of August, on Mottram Moor. In the course of a week, the resolution had been passed in nearly all the great towns of Lancashire, and tens of thousands had held up their hands in favour of it. . . .

I passed to and fro, and from and to my inn, and into the streets, viewing the town of Hanley as having become a human desert. Scarcely a person could be seen in the streets; all the works were closed, and the shops shut. I went again to my inn and wrote a letter to Leicester, telling our committee that they must get the people into the market-place and propose the Resolution to work no more till the Charter became the law of the land. Then there was the sudden thought that I must not send such a letter through the post-office. A Chartist came into the inn whom the landlord said I might trust; and he offered to start and walk to Leicester with the letter at once. . . .

The day wore on, wearily, and very anxiously, till about five in the afternoon, when parties of men began to pass along the streets. Some came into my inn, and began to relate the history of the doings at Longton, which had been violent indeed. Yet the accounts they gave were confused, and I still had no clear understanding of what had been done. . . .

Samuel Bevinton was the strongest-minded man among the Chartists of the Potteries; and he said to me, "You had better get off to Manchester. You can do no more good here." I agreed that he was right; and two Chartist friends went out to hire a gig to enable me to get to the Whitmore station, that I might get to Manchester: there was no railway through the Potteries, at that time. But they tried in several places, and all in vain. No one would lend a gig, for it was reported that soldiers and policemen and special constables had formed a kind of cordon round the Potteries, and were stopping up every outlet. . . .

My friends had purposely conducted me through dark

streets, and led me out of Hanley in such a way that I saw neither spark, smoke, or flame. Yet the rioters were burning the houses of the Rev. Mr. Aitken and Mr. Parker, local magistrates, and the house of Mr. Forrester, agent of Lord Granville (principal owner of the collieries in the Potteries) during that night. . . .

Nor did the outbreak end with that night. Next morning thousands were again in the streets of Hanley and began to pour into the other Pottery towns from the surrounding districts. A troop of cavalry, under Major Beresford, entered the district, and the daring colliers strove to unhorse the soldiers . . . one man was killed at Burslem . . . but quiet was not restored until the day after this had been done, and scores had been apprehended and taken to prison. . . .

When I entered the railway carriage at Crewe, some who were going to the Convention recognised me,—and, among the rest, Campbell, secretary of the "National Charter Association." . . . So soon as the City of Long Chimneys came in sight, and every chimney was beheld smokeless, Campbell's face changed, and with an oath he said, "Not a single mill at work! something must come out of this and something serious too!"

In Manchester, I soon found McDouall, Leach, and Bairstow, who, together with Campbell, formed what was called "The Executive Council of the National Charter Association." . . . In the streets, there were unmistakable signs of alarm on the part of the authorities. Troops of cavalry were going up and down the principal thorough-fares, accompanied by pieces of artillery, drawn by horses. In the evening, we held a meeting in the Reverend Mr. Schofield's chapel, where O'Connor, the Executive, and a considerable number of delegates were present; and it was agreed to open the Conference, or Convention, in form, the next morning, at nine o'clock. We met at that hour, the next morning, Wednesday, the 17th of August, when James Arthur of Carlisle was elected President. There were nearly sixty delegates present; and as they rose, in quick succession, to describe the state of their

M

districts, it was evident they were, each and all, filled with the desire of keeping the people from returning to their labour. They believed the time had come for trying, successfully, to paralyse the Government. . . .

McDouall . . . hastily drew up an exciting and fiercely worded address to the working men of England, appealing to the God of Battles for the issue, and urging a universal strike. . . .

The publication of the address, with the names of the Executive appended to it, caused the police to look after them very sharply. Campbell got off to London, McDouall got away into Yorkshire, and only Leach was left at his own home in Manchester, where the police soon found him. Bairstow, I took back with me to Leicester. We walked through Derbyshire, as far as Belper, and then took the railway.

I found Leicester in a state of terror and discouragement. Before my letter from Hanley reached them, the working men had taken their own resolution, and held a meeting in the market-place, declaring their adherence to the strike which had commenced in Lancashire. They then withdrew to an elevation in the neighbourhood of Leicester, which bears the singular name of "Momecker Hill." Here they were charged by the county police, and dispersed. It often causes a laugh in Leicester, to the present time, when old Chartist days are mentioned, and some one says, "Were you at the Battle of Momecker Hill?"

Laughter was not perceptible in Leicester, when I re-entered it. The police, I was told, had charged the people in the streets, as well as upon Momecker Hill, and smitten and injured several with their staves. I called Chartist friends together, with great difficulty; and endeavoured to reassure them. And then I issued a printed address to the magistrates of Leicester, boldly reprehending them for dispersing the people; and assuring them that I should still contend for the People's Charter.

I had not been one week at home, before the Leicester police came, and handcuffed me, and took me to the

Town Hall. . . . I was handed over to the constable of Hanley, who had come to apprehend me. We reached Hanley at night, and I was taken to a "Lock-up," where a large, coarse fellow, who was set to watch over me, put huge iron bolts on my ancles, so that I could not sleep as I lay in my clothes on a board. The next day I was taken to Newcastle-under-Lyme, and brought before Mr. Mainwairing and Mr. Ayshford Wyse, magistrates.

b) MANIFESTO OF THE NATIONAL CHARTISTS' ASSOCIATION, AUGUST, 1842

Brother Chartists . . . we have solemnly sworn, and one and all declared, that the golden opportunity now within our grasp shall not pass away fruitless . . . but that we now do universally resolve never to resume labour until labour's grievances are destroyed, and protection secured for ourselves, our suffering wives, and helpless children, by the enactment of the People's Charter.

Englishmen! the blood of your brethren reddens the streets of Preston and Blackburn, and the murderers thirst for more. Be firm—be courageous—be men. Peace, law, and order, have prevailed on our side; let them be revered, until your brethren in Scotland, Wales, and Ireland, are informed of your resolution; and when a universal holiday prevails—which will be the case in eight days—then of what use will bayonets be against public opinion? What tyrant can then live above the terrible tide of thought and energy, which is now flowing fast under the guidance of man's intellect—which is now destined by the Creator to elevate his people above the reach of want, the rancour of despotism, and the penalties of bondage? The trades—a noble, patriotic band—have taken the lead in declaring for the Charter. . . . Follow their example. Lend no whip to rulers wherewith to scourge you. Intelligence has reached us of the wide spreading of the strike, and, now, within 50 miles of Manchester every engine is at rest, and all is still, save the miller's useful wheels, and friendly sickle in the fields.

Countrymen and brothers,—Centuries may roll on as

they have fleeted past, before such universal action may again be displayed. We have made the cast for liberty, and we must stand like men the hazard of the die. Let none despond. Let all be cool and watchful; and, like the bridesmaids in the parable, keep your lamps burning; and let your continued resolution be, like a beacon, to guide those who are now hastening far and wide to follow your memorable example. Brethren, we rely on your firmness. Cowardice, treachery, or womanly fear, would cast our cause back for half a century. Let no man, woman, or child, break down the solemn pledge; and if they do, may the curse of the poor and starving pursue them. They deserve slavery who would madly court it. Our machinery is all arranged, and your cause, will, in three days be impelled onward by all the intellect we can summon to its aid. Therefore, whilst you are peaceful, be firm; while you are orderly, make all be so likewise; and whilst you look to the law, remember that you had no voice in making it, and are therefore slaves to the will, the law, and the price of your masters. All officers of the Association are called upon to aid and assist in the peaceful extension of the movement, and to forward all monies for the use of the delegates who may be expressed over the country. Strengthen our hands at this crisis; support your leaders; rally round our sacred cause; and leave the decision to the "God of justice and of battle."

c) SPEECH OF RICHARD PILLING TO THE COURT

. . . Gentlemen of the jury, it is stated by one of the witnesses, that I was the father of this great movement—the father of this outbreak; if so, then punish me, and let all the rest go free. But I say it is not *me* that is the father of this movement; but that House. Our addresses have been laid before that House, and they have not redressed our grievances; and from there, and there alone, the cause comes. . . . Gentlemen, I am somewhere about 43 years of age. I was asked last night if I were not sixty. But if I had as good usage as others, instead of looking like a man of sixty, I should look something like a man of 36. I have

gone to be a hand-loom weaver, when I was about ten
years of age—in 1810. The first week I ever worked in my
life, I earned 16/– a week by the hand-loom. I followed
that occupation till 1840. . . . In 1840 I could only earn
. . . 6/6; but I should do that or become a pauper. . . .
But although I detested the factory system, yet, sooner
than become a pauper on the parish I submitted. . . .

After working in the factory seven years, a reduction
began to creep in, one way or the other. . . . I became an
opponent to the reduction of wages to the bottom of my
soul; and as long as I live I shall continue to keep up the
wages of labour, to the utmost of my power. For taking
that part in Stockport, and being the means of preventing
many reductions, the masters combined all as one man
against me, and neither me nor my children could get
a day's employment. In 1840, there was a great turn-out
in Stockport, in which turn-out I took a conspicuous part.
We were out eight weeks. We were up every morning from
five to six o'clock. Upwards of 6,000 power-loom weavers
were engaged in that turn-out. We had our processions.
We went to Ashton, Hyde, and Duckinfield in procession.
We had our processions in Manchester, and all over the
country, and we were not interfered with. . . .

We were never told at this time that we were doing
that which was wrong. Considering, from the act of
Parliament that was passed when the Combination Laws
were repealed in 1825, that I had a right to do so; I did
believe, as an Englishman, and factory operative that, in
consequence of that act, I had a right to do all that ever
lay in my power to keep up wages. In 1840 the master
manufacturers, to the number of about forty, had a
meeting, and they conspired together—if there is conspiracy on the one side there is conspiracy on the other—
and they gave us notice for a reduction of one penny
a cut. Some people think a penny is a small reduction,
but it amounts to five week's wages in the course of a
year. . . . Not content with that reduction, about twelve
months after they took off another penny a cut, besides
taking 2/– off the Throstle spinners who had only 9/–

a week, and 1/6 off the card spinners, who had only 8/- a week, and so on. When they took the other penny a cut off, I pulled all the hands out, and we went round again to all the manufacturing districts, and brought things to a level again. The manufacturers of Stockport met again, and said—"we cannot compete with Blackburn and Preston, and we must reduce again,"—and this is the way they will go on until at length they reduce so low that we shall all become paupers. . . .

In Ashton-under-Lyne one pennyworth of damage was not done to property, although we were out for six weeks . . . it was then a hard case for me to support myself and family. My eldest son but one, who was 16 years of age, had fallen into a consumption last Easter and left his work. We were then reduced to $9\frac{3}{4}d$. a cut, which brought our earnings down to something like 16/- a week. That is all I had to live on, with my nine in family, 3/- a week going out of that for rent, and a sick son lying helpless before me. I have gone home and seen that son—— (Here Pilling was moved to tears, and unable to proceed for some time.) I have seen that son lying on a sick bed and dying pillow, and having nothing to eat but potatoes and salt . . . with neither medical aid, nor any of the common necessaries of life. Yea, I recollect someone going to a gentlemen's house in Ashton, to ask for a bottle of wine for him; and it was said, "Oh, he is a chartist, he must have none." (Great sensation in court.) Oh, such usage from the rich will never convince the chartists that they are wrong. Gentlemen, my son died before the commencement of the strike; and such was the feeling of the people of Ashton towards my family, that they collected £4 towards his burial. . . . It was under these circumstances that I happened to call at Stockport— excited I will admit by the loss of my son, together with a reduction of 25%; for I will acknowledge and confess before you . . . that before I would have lived to submit to another reduction of 25%, I would have terminated my own existence. That was my intention.

Let us now come to the facts of the case. I will tell you

what was the origin of the strike. . . . Mr. Rayners of Ashton had given notice . . . that he would reduce 25%. So indignant were the feelings of the people of Ashton and the surrounding district, not only the chartists, but all sorts assembled; a room that would hold a thousand people was crammed to suffocation, and the whole voice of the meeting was, that it was of no use trying to get up a subscription for others, but to give up. And that was just the way the strike began; it rose in a minute from one end of the room to the other; whigs, tories, chartists, sham radicals, and all sorts. . . .

Well, we had a turn-out to prevent a reduction; and when Rayner saw the spirit of the meeting he withdrew his reduction. A meeting was then called at Stalybridge, and everyone withdrew the reduction except Bayley. Now, if there is one man who ought to stand here as a defendant that is the man. If he had withdrawn the reduction there would have been no strike; the people would have settled down and enjoyed a glorious triumph in preventing the reduction. A meeting was also held at Hyde; and the people of Hyde declared that if the masters attempted to make another reduction they (the working people) would give over. At Droylsden the same. This is the history of the turn-out. I would say to the jury and the people assembled here, that if it had not been for the late struggle I firmly believe thousands would have been starved to death. . . .

I was 20 years among the hand-loom weavers, and 10 years in a factory, and I unhesitatingly say, that during the whole course of that time I worked 12 hours a day with the exception of 12 months that the masters of Stockport would not employ me; and the longer and harder I have worked the poorer and poorer I have become every year, until, at last, I am nearly exhausted. If the masters had taken off another 25 $p. c.$ I would put an end to my existence sooner than kill myself working 12 hours a day in a cotton factory, and eating potatoes and salt. Gentlemen of the jury, I now leave my case in your hands. . . .

53. THE NEW MOVE, 1842

The New Move was an attempt of certain radicals to organise the workers under middle-class leadership, in a "Complete Suffrage Movement." The Chartists refused to give up their independence, though co-operation with the "Complete Suffragists" and their leader, the Quaker, Joseph Sturge, followed. From the *British Statesman*, December 31st, 1842.

Resolution of the Complete Suffrage Conference, December, 1842:

"That this conference . . . having for its paramount object the consideration of the necessary details of a bill embodying the principles . . . extension of the suffrage to all male adults . . . vote by ballot, equal electoral districts, abolition of a property qualification for M.P.s, payment of members . . . and annual Parliaments, do now declare its adoption of these principles; pledges itself to employ such means . . . as are of a strictly just, peaceful, legal and constitutional character. . . ."

Amendment moved by William Lovett; seconded by Feargus O'Connor:

"That the document entitled the People's Charter . . . having been before the public for the last five years has, in the opinion of this meeting, a prior claim over all other documents professing to embrace the principles of just representation. . . ."

[A vote was taken]   For the Complete Suffrage Bill 94
For Mr. Lovett's Amendment 193

54. THE CHARTISTS AND THE CORN LAWS

The following documents illustrate the general attitude of the Chartists to the middle-class Anti-Corn Law League. In the 1840's the controversy between both bodies was bitter. The 1845 resolution indicates a change of attitude owing to the distress of the time, but the wording is very guarded, and indicates at best "neutrality" towards Repeal. Sources of extracts: *a*) *Charter*, February 17th, 1839; *b*) Thomas Cooper *op. cit.*, pp. 136–7; *c*) *Northern Star*, December 27th, 1845.

a) RESOLUTION OF THE CHARTIST CONVENTION, 1839

THE Convention is convinced that at the present eventful crisis it is indispensably necessary to the success of the National Petition that the people's undivided attention should be concentrated upon that question to the exclusion of all others not auxiliary to the same, being also convinced that the present agitation for a repeal of the Corn Laws was intended, and does actually tend to divert the working classes from that paramount object; and being further of opinion that such an unconditional repeal as would alone be likely to receive the sanction of the Anti-Corn Law agitator would be rather injurious than otherwise to the interests of the poorer classes: we, the delegates of the Convention do, therefore, most earnestly recommend our constituents in particular and the unrepresented classes in general to deprecate and oppose all and every agitation for a repeal of the Corn Laws until the fate of the National Petition and People's Charter shall have been determined; so far as the legislature is competent to determine it.

b) SPEECH OF JOHN MASON, 1841

Not that Corn Law Repeal is wrong . . . when we get the Charter, we will repeal the Corn Laws and all the other bad laws. But if you give up your agitation for the

Charter to help the Free Traders, they will not help you
to get the Charter. Don't be deceived by the middle
classes again. You helped them to get their votes—you
swelled their cry of "The Bill, the whole Bill, and nothing
but the Bill!" But where are the fine promises they made
you? Gone to the winds! They said when they had gotten
their votes they would help you to get yours. But they
and the rotten Whigs have never remembered you. Muni-
cipal Reform has been for their benefit—not for yours.
All other reforms the Whigs boast to have effected have
been for the benefit of the middle classes—not for yours.
And now they want to get the Corn Laws repealed—not
for your benefit—but for their own. "Cheap bread," they
cry. But they mean "Low wages." Do not listen to their
cant and humbug. Stick to your Charter. You are veritable
slaves without your votes!

c) RESOLUTION OF THE CHARTIST CONVENTION, 1845

That while the present scarcity would place the Chartist
party in a false position if they continued their opposition
to the repeal of the Corn Laws, that, nevertheless, having
no faith whatever in the efficacy of that measure, as a
means of bettering the condition of the working classes,
that we abstain from taking any part calculated to make
our approval of the principles of free trade, without
political power being conferred upon the whole people
to make the change a national instead of a class benefit.

That in order to carry out the spirit of the resolution,
we recommend the Chartist party to abstain from taking
any part in free trade meetings that are held for the
purpose of repealing the Corn Laws. . . .

That in the event of public meetings being called to
test public opinion, it will be the bounden duty of the
Chartist party to move their principles as an amendment
to any proposition calculated to lead to the notion that
Chartism has been merged in any less measure.

THE CHARTIST LAND PLAN, 1845

After the defeats of 1842, O'Connor turned to schemes of co-operative land settlement. The plan first mooted in 1843 languished at first. After reconstitution, the National Co-operative Land Society became the National Land Company early in 1847, with the object of buying estates and dividing them into smallholdings. The price of shares was reduced to 26s. Settlement was by ballot among the shareholders. Five settlements, including O'Connorville, near Watford, Herts, were established by the end of 1848, when, though about 75,000 working people had joined the Company, its affairs had to be wound up. Extract from the *Northern Star*, May 3rd, 1845. For O'Connor see No. 39 note.

The Convention of the Industrious Classes to the people of the United Kingdom

WE have prepared a plan, which we now submit to your earnest attention, for facilitating your location on the land. The land being the raw material of all wealth, it is essential you should practically be convinced of the inestimable value of its possession.

RULES AND REGULATIONS OF THE CHARTIST LAND CO-OPERATIVE SOCIETY

To consist of an unlimited number of Shareholders.
Shares £2 10s. each.
To be paid in weekly settlements of 3/6d., 1/– and upwards.

OBJECTS OF THE SOCIETY

To purchase land on which to locate such of its members as may be selected for that purpose, in order to demonstrate to the working classes of the kingdom,—firstly, the value of the land as a means of making them independent of the grinding capitalists; and, secondly, to show them the necessity of securing the speedy enactment of the People's

Charter, which would do for them nationally what the society proposes to do sectionally: the accomplishment of the political and social emancipation of the enslaved and degraded working classes being the peculiar object of the society.

MEANS: Good arable land may be rented in some of the most fertile parts of the country at the rate of 15/- per acre, and might be bought at 25 years' purchase, that is at £18-15s. per acre. And supposing £5,000 raised . . . this sum would purchase 120 acres and locate 60 persons with two acres each, besides leaving a balance of £2,750 which would give to each of the occupants £45-16s.-8d., £30 of which would be sufficient to build a commodious and comfortable cottage on each allotment; one half of the remaining £15-16s.-8d. would be sufficient to purchase implements, stock, etc. leaving the residue as a means of subsistence for the occupants until his allotment produced the necessaries of life. These allotments, with dwellings, might be *leased for ever* to the members of the society at an annual rental of £5 each, which would be below their real value. The gross annual rental would thus amount to £300. This property, if sold at 20 years purchase (which would be far below the market value) would yield the funds of the society £6,000, which sum if expended in a similar manner to the first, would locate other 72 persons on two acres of land, provided with *homes*. These 72 allotments sold at the rate of the first, would bring £7,200; and this sum laid out in the purchase of other land, building of cottages etc. at the original rate, would locate 86 and two-fifths persons. These 86 two-fifths allotments, if sold, would realise £8,634-8s.; and with this amount of capital the society could locate other 103 one-sixth persons. These 103 one-sixth allotments would produce £10,317-3s.-4d.; and the last named sum, expended as before would locate 123 one-third persons. Thus the original capital of £5,000, would more than double itself at the fourth sale; and so on, at the same rates . . . continuing to increase in the same proportion until the tenth sale which would realise

£37,324, and locate 372½ persons. Thus the total number which would be located in ten sales—which if the project be taken up with spirit, might easily be effected in four years—would be 1,923 persons; in addition to leaving in possession of the society an estate worth at least, in the wholesale market, £37,324, which estate could be resold, increasing at each sale in value and capability of sustaining the members, until in the space of a few years a vast number of the "surplus labour population" could be placed in happiness and prosperity upon the soil of their native land, and thus become valuable consumers as well as producers of wealth. . . .

56. AGAINST UTOPIAN SOCIALISM

From the *National Reformer and Manx Weekly Review*, edited by Bronterre O'Brien, January 30th, 1847.

THE systems of Owen, Fourier, St. Simon, etc., transcend the capabilities of all human legislature, and may . . . be incompatible with the essential character of man, and therefore impossible of realisation on a universal scale. Mr. O'Brien demands for the people only those fundamental rights, political and social, to which they are as clearly entitled as they are to the right of existence; and in favour of which there would, therefore, be no difficulty in setting up a sound public opinion amongst nine tenths of the people. . . . But it would be perfectly impossible to establish a general public opinion in favour of Owenism, which exists only in one man's imagination. . . . The people's rights once established, and proper laws acted upon Land, Currency, Credit and Exchange, an unbounded field of progressive improvement and prosperity would thenceforward lie open to the people. Free in all their thoughts and actions they would soon discover what wonders in production, and in distribution, and in the sciences generally, might be achieved by Associative labour, in comparison with the exertions of isolated individual labour.

Thence would gradually arise the true social state,—the realities of socialism, as contra distinguished from the present dreams about it. And doubtless the ultimate consequences would be the universal prevalence of a state of society not essentially different from that conceived by Owen. . . . But the idea of jumping at once from our present iniquitous, corrupt state of society into . . . social paradises, without any previous recognition of human rights and without the establishment of a single law or institution to rescue the people from their present brutalised state of ignorance and vassalage, is a most perfect chimera.

57. ERNEST JONES: ELECTION ADDRESS, HALIFAX, 1847

Ernest Jones (1819–69) was born of upper-class parents. Converted to Chartism in 1845, his rise to leadership was meteoric. He became an editor of the *Northern Star*, was renowned as a poet and orator and imprisoned for two years for his part in the events of 1848 (No. 59). His greatest activity was after this period. (See Vol. II in this series.) At the general election of 1847, for which this Halifax address was written, Jones polled 279 votes; the lowest successful candidate polled 506. Extract from the *Northern Star*, July 3rd, 1847.

I SOLICIT your support as an advocate of the following reforms: . . . Universal Suffrage . . . Vote by Ballot . . . Annual Parliaments . . . No Property Qualification . . . Payment of Members . . . Equal Electoral Districts . . . The Separation of Church and State . . . The restoration of that portion of Church Property taken from the poor to its rightful owners . . . A Voluntary System of Education . . . without any Government interference or control. . . .

The abolition of Capital Punishments . . . The abolition of the New Poor Law . . . The repeal of the laws of Primogeniture and Entail . . . The repeal of the Game Laws . . . A system of Direct Taxation . . . An extension of the small Proprietary System by means of Government support, for reclaiming waste lands and the purchase of land for the people . . . A consistent development of . . . Free Trade, by a repeal of the Navigation laws and other monopolies pressing on the mechanical and agricultural industry of the country.

I shall feel it my duty annually to present myself before the inhabitants of your borough, in public meeting assembled, and there to resign my trust into their hands should such be the will of the majority. . . .

58. FEARGUS O'CONNOR: NOTTINGHAM ELECTION, 1847

Feargus O'Connor's Address after his election for Nottingham, 1847. *Northern Star*, August 7th, 1847. For his change in tone, compare No. 39.

To the Independent Electors of Nottingham.

. . . Gentlemen, I do not despise a rich man because he is rich, any more than I despise a poor man because he is poor; and therefore I wage no battle against wealth which is fairly and honourably accumulated, while I war against a system which enables idlers to live upon the labour of the industrious.

Gentlemen, one mode by which I propose to equalise society is, by the annihilation of all those duties and taxes which press upon the industrious portion of society, whether employers or employed. I shall make it my study to reduce the taxation of the country to that point which will preserve harmony amongst all classes, and substitute a moral for a physical force government.

To give the people a good education, uninterfered with by any religious domination, shall be one of my primary objects. . . . You will not find me the rash and headstrong Destructive that I have been represented . . . for I would not owe my liberty to the shedding of a drop of human blood. . . .

While the wealthy are traversing the world in search of foreign . . . trade, it is my aim and object to create for you a home trade, through the ability of your own people to traffic with you. . . . This I seek to accomplish by making the natural labourer producer of your food and consumer of the artificial labourer's produce. I seek to make machinery tributary to man's wants and not the controller of his household. . . .

I am for national, not mere class Free Trade, and the benefit that I seek from it for labour is its total emancipation from the possibility of idleness and the chance of casual dependence.

In conclusion, gentlemen, I am for the altar, for the Throne and for the cottage; but I wish to see the altar the footstool of God, instead of the couch of Mammon. I wish to see the Throne supported upon the affections of the people, instead of upon the caprice of an oligarchy— and I wish to see the cottage the castle of the freeman instead of the den of the slave. . . .

59. THE MOVEMENT IN THE COUNTRY, MARCH, 1848

From Gammage, *op. cit.*, pp. 315–18.

THE distress that existed was terrible—men could scarcely be worse off. Starvation glared from the eyes of thousands. . . . In the provinces, things began to look very threatening. At Glasgow the most dire distress prevailed. On the 6th of March, a serious riot took place. The unemployed operatives had expected a distribution of provisions, which, however, did not take place. In a starving condition, and writhing under their cruel disappointment, they proceeded up Irongate and other principal streets, breaking into the provision and gun shops. It was only thieves and similar characters that helped themselves to anything more than necessity required. Business was suspended. The shops were shut. The people marched through the streets, crying "Bread or Revolution!" The police were almost useless, and the military were called out. The riot act was read, but in the meantime other bodies of people proceeded in different directions, entering the provision shops, and demanding bread. The excitement became so great, that the authorities sent to Edinburgh for more troops. On the following day, crowds again collected at Bridgeton, where the out pensioners were under arms. A boy threw a clod at one of these: he was arrested. A rescue was effected, when Captain Smart, Superintendent of Police, gave orders to fire. The result of this precipitate order was that five persons were shot, and some of them died upon the spot. The military continued to parade the streets, which were still lined with people, and all the public offices were strictly guarded.

At Manchester, the people met in front of the Union Workhouse, Tile-street, and demanded the release of the inmates. The police marched in a strong body to the spot, but it was seven o'clock in the evening before they could disperse the crowd, having been engaged in the conflict for four hours. Later in the evening, the people attacked the police station in the Oldham road, put out the lamps in that neighbourhood, broke up the stalls in Smithfield Market, with which they armed themselves, and attacked the police. The military were kept under arms, and the magistrates sat at the Town-Hall, ready to act in case of emergency.

O'Connor entered Hanley, in the Potteries, on the 6th of March. A tremendous procession escorted him into the town. 2,000 people sat down with him to tea in the Covered Market, after which the people were admitted, when not less than 7,000 people were addressed by the great Chartist chief. Newcastle, Dumfries, Sunderland, Bath, Nottingham, and a host of towns were roused at the summons of the people of Paris. Public meetings were held, and the spark of democracy seemed to light up every breast. At Carlisle, an election took place for the representation of the city. The Chartists put forward Dr. M'Douall, who was carried by a tremendous show of hands, went to the poll, and polled 55 against 414 votes. This mockery of representation must be noted, in order to show posterity the wide disparity between the electoral and non-electoral bodies in the enlightened nineteenth century.

In Dublin, John Mitchell started a paper, under the title of the *United Irishman*. It breathed vengeance against the English Government, and gave plain instructions on street warfare, showing that every woman might be a soldier, by throwing bottles and other missiles, and even vitriol on the troops.

The Chartist Executive summoned a Convention, to meet in London on the 3rd of April. The following week brought no cessation of agitation. A great meeting was held on Kennington Common, on the 13th of March. There were about 20,000 persons present. 400 police were in attendance; 80 were mounted and armed with sabres and pistols, who amused themselves with riding about the Common. Numbers of the force were scattered through the meeting, dressed in plain clothes. Special constables were sworn in. The gun-makers were requested by the authorities to unscrew the barrels of their fire-arms, and the dealers in powder and shot were ordered to be cautious in the sale of those articles. The tri-colour waved from the hustings on which the speakers were assembled. Mr. Reynolds presided, and the mass were addressed by Messrs. McGrath, Williams, Clark, Dixon, and Ernest Jones, who delivered a most thrilling speech. The meeting unanimously adopted the Charter.

60. THE CHARTIST CONVENTION, APRIL, 1848

Before the third Chartist Petition was presented (April 10th, 1848), London had been turned into an armed camp, thousands of special constables sworn in and troops assembled under the Duke of Wellington. Extract *a*) is a resolution passed by the Chartist Convention on April 3rd, 1848; *b*) is the Address issued by the Convention after the events of April 10th, when the petition was again rejected. See Introduction, p. 28. The "National Assembly" was eventually held by a small number of Chartists on May 1st. *a*) is from Gammage, *op. cit.*, p. 331; *b*) from the *Northern Star*, April 15th, 1848.

a) RESOLUTION OF THE CONVENTION

1st.—That in the event of the National Petition being rejected by the House of Commons, this Convention prepare a National Memorial to the Queen to dissolve the present Parliament, and call to her council such ministers only as will make the People's Charter a cabinet measure.

2nd.—That this Convention agree to the convocation of a National Assembly, to consist of delegates appointed at public meetings, to present the National Memorial to the Queen, and to continue permanently sitting until the Charter is the law of the land.

3rd.—That this Convention call upon the country to hold simultaneous meetings on Good Friday, April 21st, for the purpose of adopting the National Memorial, and electing delegates to the National Assembly.

4th.—That the National Assembly meet in London on April 24th.

5th.—That the present Convention shall continue its sittings until the meeting of the National Assembly.

b) ADDRESS OF THE CONVENTION

The legal and constitutional rights of Englishmen have been interfered with. . . . We announced a peaceful unarmed demonstration. . . . But how were these proceedings met? By the revival of an Act passed in the time of a libidinous tyrant, Charles the Second, an act 200 years old, long deemed obsolete, and indeed virtually repealed by the Bill of Rights. . . .

On Monday a procession repaired from the Convention Hall to Kennington Common, where a quarter of a million votaries of freedom were assembled. An intimation was then conveyed to us that no procession could be allowed to recross the river. We found that we were caught in a trap, that the bridges were closed against us, and that the vile proclamation of the government had been backed by warlike preparations on a scale so vast, that it appeared as if a hostile armament of 200,000 men were about to besiege the metropolis. . . . Under these circumstances we felt ourselves constrained to embrace one of these two alternatives,—either to bring an unarmed people into collision with an armed authority . . . or to leave the odium on the government of having prevented by a sanguinary prohibition, the exercise of an undoubted right.

We chose the latter course. . . .

Fellow countrymen! The first victory is gained. The courage of the men of London has been tested—despite the government prohibition, they came together in such numbers as the metropolis has never before witnessed. . . . This has been the first step; let the country prepare for the next. The duty of the Convention will be . . . to organise the people for the second and more decisive effort. . . . The National Assembly will meet on the 24th of the month. . . . The country must be prepared to support the resolve of that—the people's parliament. . . .

61. CHARTISM AND THE TRADE UNIONS

From the *Northern Star*, November 16th, 1844. By Feargus
O'Connor.

I INVITE you to keep your eye steadily fixed upon the
great Trades' Movement now manifesting itself throughout the country, and I would implore you to act by all
other trades as you have acted by the Colliers. Attend
their meetings, swell their numbers, and give them your
sympathy; but on no account interpose the Charter as
an obstacle to their proceedings. All labour and all labourers
must unite; and they will speedily discover that the
Charter is the only standard under which they can successfully rally. . . .

62. NORTHUMBERLAND AND DURHAM MINERS, 1844

Extracts *a*) to *d*) from *The Miners of Northumberland and Durham* by Richard Fynes, 1873, and *e*) from *The Condition of the Working Class in England in 1844*, by Frederick Engels, describe the background and events of the miners' strike of 1844. *a*) Fynes, p. 52, a miners' petition to Parliament; *b*) p. 54, Correspondence on grievances; *c*) p. 54, Resolution passed at the "Conference of the Miners' Association of Great Britain and Ireland"; *d*) p. 57, from the speech of Mark Dent, Chairman, Northumberland and Durham Miners, at a strike demonstration on Shadon's Hill; *e*) From Engels' *Condition of the Working Class in England in 1844*, pp. 255-7. (This work was first published in Germany, 1845.) The "Attorney-General" referred to on p. 204 was W. P. Roberts, famous as a lawyer who defended the trade unions.

a) THAT your petitioners, miners of the coal and other mines of Great Britain and Ireland, have, by sad and manifold experience, been subject to frequent disastrous explosions of inflammable gas whilst following their respective employments, which have been invariably attended with great sacrifice of human life, and consequently entailing a serious and extensive amount of privation and misery. . . .

That your Honourable House would be pleased to enact and appoint inspectors of mines (as of factories) to see to the safety of ropes and other machinery connected with the danger of life and property, also to inspect the ventilation at proper periods, so as to prevent the recurrence of explosion, partial or extensive. . . .

That your Honourable House would cause to be enacted a law compelling proper weighing machines, on the beam and scale principle, so that your petitioners may have the produce of their labour accurately weighed, and such weighing machines to be under the surveillance of the proper authorities, and subject to be tested and adjusted by them, without notice, at all seasonable times, with a power to remove and condemn the same if found defective.

That your Honourable House would enact and pass into law, that the wages earned by your petitioners be paid weekly and up to the last work performed, with the exception of one day allowed for the making up the accounts thereof.

b) EXTRACTS FROM CORRESPONDENCE

WEST HOLYWELL COLLIERY.—We work the tubs at 4½*d.* per tub, and when the tubs are laid out, we are fined 6*d.*, and paid nothing for hewing the coals. They fine us for sending small coals to bank, at the same time they are selling them for 6*s.* per chaldron.

ELEMORE COLLIERY.—The rule at this colliery is to pay fortnightly every Friday. Last pay-day they would not pay us on the Friday, but they said they would pay us next morning. We went for our money at 7 o'clock in the morning and we were kept waiting till 5 o'clock in the afternoon, while they knew our wives had a great way to go to buy a bit of meat. The viewer at this colliery was not very long ago a coal hewer. He appears to have forgot himself. Oh God! how long are the miners to suffer this oppression?

TYNE MAIN COLLIERY.—The laid out is something fearful here. A man sent nine corves to bank, eight of them were laid out because they were not chalked. He is a hewer in a place two yards wide. One part of the place was bright coal, and the other, rusty. When the overman came into the place, he asked him what he was to do, he said he really did not know, but he might do so and so, "but do not say that I told." Now, what is the man to do, when the masters do not know. When the coals were rusty the man was to chalk them; when bright, he had not to do so. This man worked for 1/6 and there was 2/– kept off him; so that he laboured all day for nothing, and had to pay the masters 6*d.* for allowing him to do so. Kind Heaven look down upon us, and guide us the way to get clear of this oppression, for the miners cup is about full. No human being can bear the treatment which is daily inflicted upon us!

c) RESOLUTION OF CONFERENCE

It is the decision of this committee that the men of Northumberland and Durham ought, after using every other lawful means, and not yet gaining their end, to be allowed to refuse to work under the masters' agreement, which is to take place on the 5th day of April next; and we, the delegates from the different parts of the kingdom, do hereby pledge ourselves to do all in our power to assist them in their struggle, and also to prevent men from coming in amongst them; and, if possible, still further to restrict our labour.

d) SPEECH OF MR. MARK DENT

Fellow men, we have long been divided, but I hope this day is the uniting of the miners of the Tees, Wear and Tyne for the purpose of having our grievances adjusted, for they are manifold and severe. We have long sought for redress, we have been treated with scorn, but now we are resolved to be free. We are an insulted, oppressed, and degraded body of men. . . . Miners as a class are not looked on with respect by the public, and the great majority of the press seems to be against us. Our employers use every means to oppress us, and this is not to be wondered at, for we have had no respect for ourselves. But now that there is an understanding amongst us, are we any longer to continue to drag the chains of slavery, to bear the yokes of bondage and toil in the bowels of the earth, as we have done?

e) THE STORY OF THE STRIKE, TOLD BY FREDERICK ENGELS

. . . Meanwhile the strike in the North was proceeding. Not a hand stirred, and Newcastle, the chief coal port, was so stripped of its commodity that coal had to be brought from the Scotch coast, in spite of the proverb. At first, while the Union's funds held out, all went well, but towards summer the struggle became much more

painful for the miners. The greatest want prevailed
among them; they had no money, for the contributions
of the workers of all branches of industry in England
availed little among the vast number of strikers, who
were forced to borrow from the small shopkeepers at a
heavy loss. The whole press, with the single exception of
the few proletarian journals, was against them; the bourgeois, even the few among them who might have had
enough sense of justice to support the miners, learnt from
the corrupt Liberal and Conservative sheets only lies
about them. A deputation of twelve miners who went to
London received a sum from the proletariat there, but
this too, availed little among the mass who needed support. Yet, in spire of all this, the miners remained steadfast, and what is even more significant, were quiet and
peaceable in the face of all the hostilities and provocation
of the mine owners and their faithful servants. No act of
revenge was carried out, not a renegade was maltreated,
not one single theft committed.

Thus the strike had continued well on towards four
months, and the mine owners still had no prospect of
getting the upper hand. One way was, however, still open
to them. They remembered the cottage system; it occurred
to them that the houses of the rebellious spirits were
THEIR property. In July, notice to quit was served the
workers, and, in a week, the whole forty thousand were
put out of doors. This measure was carried out with
revolting cruelty. The sick, the feeble, old men and little
children, even women in childbirth were mercilessly
turned from their beds and cast into the roadside ditches.
One agent dragged by the hair from her bed, and into
the street, a woman in the pangs of childbirth. Soldiers
and police in crowds were present, ready to fire at the
first symptom of resistance, on the slightest hint of the
Justices of the Peace, who had brought about the whole
brutal procedure. This, too, the working-men endured
without resistance. The hope had been that the men
would use violence; they were spurred on with all force
to infringements of the laws; to furnish an excuse for

making an end of the strike by the intervention of the military. The homeless miners, remembering the warnings of their Attorney General, remained unmoved, set up their household goods upon the moors or the harvested fields, and held out. Some, who had no other place, encamped on the roadsides and in ditches, others upon land belonging to other people, whereupon they were prosecuted, and, having caused "damage of the value of a halfpenny," were fined a pound, and, being unable to pay it, worked it out on the treadmill.

Thus they lived eight weeks and more of the wet fag-end of last summer under the open sky with their families, with no further shelter for themselves and their little ones than the calico curtains of their beds; with no other help than the scanty allowances of their Union and the fast shrinking credit with the small dealers. Hereupon Lord Londonderry, who owns considerable mines in Durham, threatened the small tradesmen in "his" town of Seaham with his most high displeasure if they should continue to give credit to "his" rebellious workers. This "noble" lord made himself the first clown of the turnout in consequence of the ridiculous, pompous, ungrammatical ukases addressed to the workers, which he published from time to time, with no other result than the merriment of the nation. When none of their efforts produced any effect, the mine owners imported, at great expense, hands from Ireland and such remote parts of Wales as have as yet no labour movement. And when the competition of workers against workers was thus restored, the strength of the strikers collapsed. The mine owners obliged them to renounce the Union, abandon Roberts, and accept the conditions laid down by the employers. Thus ended at the close of September the great five months' battle of the coal miners against the mine owners, a battle fought on the part of the oppressed with an endurance, courage, intelligence, and coolness which demands the highest admiration. . . .

63. NATIONAL TRADES UNION CONFERENCE

NATIONAL ASSOCIATION OF UNITED TRADES, 1845

This inaugural Conference was attended by 110 delegates.
Keen discussion occurred on the proposal for local Boards of
Trade. The Chairman was Thomas Duncombe, M.P., who
had moved the second Chartist Petition in Parliament in
1842 (No. 50), and was closely associated with the Trade
Union movement of the period. The *Northern Star* gave
regular space to the activities of the new organisation, which
continued a lingering existence until 1867. Extract from the
Northern Star, March 29th, 1845. See Introduction, p. 28.

a) REPORT OF THE LONDON COMMITTEE OF TRADES DELEGATES
TO THE GENERAL CONFERENCE

THE Committee . . . are deeply impressed with the
importance of, and benefit arising from, good understanding between the employer and employed, seeing
that their interests are to some extent mutual . . . they,
therefore, would suggest that it should be one of the
principal objects of the Conference to cultivate a good
understanding with the employers. . . . Although the
Committee are anxious that this desirable and important
organisation should be carried out to the fullest possible
extent, they feel that great caution must be observed in
the formation of its laws and regulations, in order that
the evils which existed, and eventually destroyed the consolidated Union of 1833 shall be carefully avoided. . . .
Finally the Committee would earnestly recommend . . .
that no proposition of a political nature, beyond what has been
already alluded to, should be introduced to occupy its
attention . . . to keep trade matters and politics as
separate and distinct as circumstances will justify.

b) REPORT ADOPTED BY THE CONFERENCE

. . . The primary object of all Trades' Unions is to
secure to the Operative a fair and just participation in the
wealth he assists to produce. For some years past an
opinion has been gradually gaining ground among these

bodies that their organisation and the application of their funds heretofore, have neither been the best nor the most effective that might have been adopted. Repeated failure has induced scepticism as to the efficacy of STRIKES ALONE to protect the labourers from the aggression of Capital, and to arrest that downward tendency, which is the most prominent feature of his condition. At the same time, increased experience and information has excited a desire amongst some of the Trades, to attempt Association on a larger scale for the protection of industry; or at least to *deliberate* whether there may not be a better method of applying the large sums annually collected for the use of these societies.

. . . The working classes must summon to their aid those appliances which have hitherto principally been employed against them. They must expend their funds— locally or generally—in the erection of machines that will work *for* and not *against* them; and instead of investing funds with bankers, to be used by large capitalists, in a way which inevitably lowers the condition of the con- tributors, they must apply them to the production of real wealth and profitable results for themselves.

The time may not yet have arrived when practical measures for this purpose can be commended . . . the *immediate* measures which it appears to your Committee this Conference may usefully take into consideration are the following:

1. A society, to be called the Association of United Trades for the Protection of Industry. . . .

3. The leading objects of the Association may be divisible into two departments—the first external, having reference to the influence of the Legislature on the con- dition of the industrious classes; the second internal, or to efforts made by the Trades to improve their own condition.

With respect to the first of these divisions . . . the Central Committee should be . . . instructed to take every opportunity . . . to enforce the adoption of shorter hours of labour wherever practicable. . . .

4. Another measure . . . is, the establishment of Local
Boards of Trade . . . composed of masters and operatives,
to whom all matters affecting the regulation of wages,
duration of labour, disputes etc. shall be referred, and
their decisions have the authority of law . . . (. . . the
proposed Boards of Trade, being equally composed of
employers and employed, would have a tendency to
prevent strikes and turn-outs by all differences being first
submitted to an impartial tribunal, and authoritatively
settled by it . . .).

5. The second division of the Association should be the
collection and diffusion of information, as to the means
by which capital, skill and labour of the Trades can be
applied for their own benefit, and especially to enable
them to abstract from the labour market and set to profitable employment, the redundant hands, who if suffered
to remain in it, would reduce the wages of the whole trade
to which they belong. . . . Your Committee recommends
that no interference be attempted with the local organisation of individual Trades; but that the new organisation
. . . be simply *an addition* . . . though they hope . . . this
addition will become so *effective* as to supersede mere
local and sectional efforts. . . .

6. The Central Committee should be instructed to
carefully prepare a plan for concentrating the energies,
legalising the proceedings, and giving practical effect to
the growing desire for location in the land. . . .

Part Six

PRODUCERS AND CONSUMERS

64. THE STRUGGLE FOR A SHORTER WORKING DAY

Owen, inspired by the success of his reforms, which made his factory at New Lanark the object of pilgrimage from all over the world, succeeded after intensive lobbying in persuading Sir Robert Peel to introduce a Factory Bill in the House of Commons. Much mutilated, it became the Factory Act of 1819. Extract *a*) is from *The Story of My Life*, by Robert Owen, 1857, pp. 116–20. The succeeding extracts illustrate the struggle between 1832 and 1848.

Sources are: *b*) *The Poor Man's Advocate* (written by J. Doherty), March 17th, 1832; *c*) *Cobbett's Weekly Political Register*, December 14th, 1833; *d*) *ibid.*, December 7th, 1833; *e*) *London Mercury*, April 2nd, 1837; *f*) *Northern Star*, December 27th, 1845; *g*) *ibid.*, January 2nd, 1847; *h*) *ibid.*, February 6th, 1847; *i*) *ibid.*, January 8th, 1848. For Doherty, see No. 16, for Fielden, No. 37.

a) OWEN AND THE FACTORY ACT OF 1819

HAD Sir Robert Peel been so inclined, he might have speedily carried this bill, as it was, through the House of Commons, during the first session. . . . But it appeared afterwards that he was too much under the influence of his brother manufacturers; and he allowed this bill, of so much real importance to the country, the master manufacturers, and the working classes, to be dragged through the House of Commons for four sessions before it was passed, and when passed it had been so mutilated in all its valuable clauses, that it became valueless for the objects I had intended. . . .

Children at this time were admitted into the cotton, wool, flax and silk mills at six, and sometimes even at five years of age. The time of working, winter and summer, was unlimited by law, but usually it was fourteen hours per day—in some fifteen, and even, by the most inhuman and avaricious, sixteen hours—and in many cases the mills were artificially heated to a high state unfavourable to health. . . .

The bill as I prepared it was assented to by all the leading members of both Houses, except the trading and manufacturing interests. . . . Sir Robert Peel, yielding to the clamour of the manufacturers, first gave up wool, flax and silk, and they were struck out at the commencement, although at that time flax spinning was the most unhealthy of the four manufactures. . . .

I sat with the Factory Committee of the House of Commons every day for two sessions, and was on one occasion examined by it as a witness in favour of the bill in its original state, limiting the time of working the mills to ten hours per day—the age of admission for children to work in them for that time, to twelve—for the boys and girls to be taught to read and write previously to their admission. . . .

My evidence as an extensive mill owner, who had in his own practice adopted these regulations in his establishment . . . had an influence not to be overcome by any ordinary or fair means . . . therefore the manufacturing members of the House . . . resorted to the most unfair means in their examination, especially Sir George Phillips . . . who . . . took upon himself to question me at great length on my religious beliefs. . . .

b) DOHERTY ON MR. SADLER'S FACTORY BILL, 1832

The question is, whether you will have a ten hours' bill or a twelve hours' bill. We say a TEN HOURS' BILL OR NO BILL AT ALL. Is any working man now debating with himself whether he would prefer a ten or twelve hours' bill? Let us ask him how much he has saved by the longest hours he ever worked? Or how much he would be able to save, were he to work sixteen, or even eighteen hours a day? Is there a working man in the country who does not now know, that be the prophets of the trade what they may, the workman is only permitted to live, no matter how many hours he may toil . . . work twelve, work twenty hours, and you must only have what will enable you to crawl on through life, a miserable dependent . . . work ten or eight hours and your condition will not be worse, but better; for not being worked till nature is exhausted, you will possess both spirit to demand, and nerve to enforce, your claim to better treatment . . . the only result of the most incessant and wasting drudgery is, increased misery and privation to the neglected, defenceless workmen. . . . Let them cease to "produce" so much, that the "demand" for their labour may increase.

c) JOHN FIELDEN TO WILLIAM COBBETT

Waterside, 16th November, 1833.

I am persuaded we are on the eve of very important changes; the working people will not long submit to the chains with which they are enthralled; co-operative societies, trades unions, etc., exist in almost every manufacturing town and village. . . .

An organisation has thus been formed; which if properly directed, may be productive of good . . . the disappointment on being denied the ten-hour bill is not yet forgotten, and active measures are now on foot to obtain by unions such regulations as to time of labour and the amount of wages as the workpeople think . . . they are fairly entitled to.

Mr. Robert Owen called on me last week; he had been amongst them in Yorkshire, recommending them how to act, if the threat of the masters to dismiss every person in their employ who would not abandon the Unions, were attempted to be carried into effect. . . .

I thought it desirable to suggest a mode of procedure on the part of the workpeople in factories, which, if successful, would supply the defect in the factory bill passed last session and do away with the necessity for further legislation on the subject.

The plan is, that about the 1st of March next the day the said bill . . . limits the work for children under eleven years of age to eight hours a day, those above that age both grown persons and adults, should insist on eight hours a day being the maximum of time for them to labour; and their present weekly wages for sixty nine hours a week, to be the minimum weekly wages for forty eight hours a week after that time.

Mr. Owen said the plan was the best he had ever suggested; it was practicable . . . and he is now at work in Yorkshire promoting the object. . . .

If the workpeople in factories cannot, by mutual protection, reduce the time of labour, and the system of relays of children be adopted, I expect to see (as I believe was the intention of the framers of the Factory bill) adults compelled to work sixteen hours a day against two sets of children working eight hours a day, each set; and rather than see this, I would, if I had the power, suspend the work in factories altogether.

. . . In little more than two years the restriction to eight hours extends to children of thirteen, and everyone who understands the subject knows that these children generally are as capable of doing the work allotted to them in factories for as long a time and with as little fatigue as the adults can do theirs. Eight hours of confinement and labour in factories per day are enough for either. The labour of eight hours now, from the increased speed of the machinery, requires as much or more exertion, as twelve hours did twenty years ago. . . .

JOHN FIELDEN.

d) SOCIETY FOR PROMOTING NATIONAL REGENERATION
Formed in Manchester. November 25th, 1833

At a meeting of the Working People of Manchester and their Friends . . . it was unanimously resolved

1. That it is desirable that all who wish to see society improved and confusion avoided, should endeavour to assist the working classes to obtain "FOR EIGHT HOURS' WORK THE PRESENT FULL DAY'S WAGES," such eight hours to be performed between the hours of six in the morning and six in the evening; and that the new

regulation should commence on the first day of March next.

2. That ... a society shall be formed ... "The Society for promoting National Regeneration."

3. That persons be immediately appointed from among the workmen to visit their fellow workmen in each trade, manufacture and employment ... for the purpose of communicating with them on the subject of the above resolutions and of inducing them to determine upon their adoption.

4. That persons be also appointed to visit the master manufacturers in each trade ... to recommend to them the adoption of the new regulation. ...

5. That all persons engaged in gratuitous education on Sundays and during the week days be respectfully invited to make arrangements for throwing open their schoolrooms to the working classes for two hours a day. ...

15. That Messrs. Oastler, Wood, Bull, Sadler and others, be urgently requested to desist from soliciting Parliament for a ten hours' bill and to use their utmost exertions in aid of the measures now adopted ... eight hours work for the present full days' wages. ...

19. That this Meeting earnestly appeal to their fellow men in France, Germany and the other countries of Europe, and on the continent of America, for their support and co-operation in this effort to improve the condition of the labourer in all parts of the world.

e) FOR A TEN HOURS' BILL, MANCHESTER, 1837

On Friday afternoon last a meeting was held in Batty's circus, Great Bridgewater St., for the purpose of petitioning Parliament for a Ten Hours Factory Bill. It was attended by nearly three thousand people, chiefly of the working classes, and lasted several hours. ... A series of resolutions were adopted, to the effect that the present system of factory labour is repugnant to every feeling of humanity and justice ... and that therefore the meeting were resolved to lessen its evils by diminishing the hours of labour to at least ten hours per day.

f) ADDRESS OF THE CHARTIST CONVENTION, 1845

. . . We likewise entreat you earnestly to pour in your petitions at the proper time to the House of Commons in favour of the Ten Hours Bill. The enactment of this most equitable measure would, we are convinced, confer manifold advantages on myriads of men, women and children whose very lives are being sacrificed by long hours and intense toil in the noxious atmosphere of the rattle box, to uphold the unhallowed luxury of the mammon-adoring capitalists. Humanity, justice and self interest, demand an abridgement of the hours of factory labour. . . .

g) DELEGATE MEETING IN MANCHESTER, 1847

The delegate of the Lancashire Central Short Time Committee moved the first resolution . . . "That this meeting of delegates from the manufacturing districts of Lancaster, York, Chester, and Derby, assembled for the purpose of promoting the Ten Hours Bill, again express our determination never to relax in our exertions until a Bill to limit the hours of Factory labour to ten hours a day for five days in the week, and eight on the Saturday, be obtained from the legislature, believing that we are justly entitled to protection to those limits."

The delegate from Littleborough moved the second resolution. "The experience of the last thirty-five years, in promoting this measure, warrants this meeting in believing that the rejection of the measure last session, and the means adopted by the Government, by which our friends in Parliament were defeated, has stimulated the Operatives throughout the Country to still further exertions than they have ever before made, and this meeting is convinced that the cause which has assembled them together is in accordance with every principle of justice, humanity and religion." . . .

The Delegate from the fine Spinners of Manchester . . . moved the third resolution. . . .

"That this meeting having heard the principles of Mr. John Fielden's Bill explained, which directs that on and after the passing of the Act all mills shall at once commence working eleven hours, and fixes the time of labour at ten hours in 1849, are willing to accept it in the terms proposed. This meeting will, therefore, on behalf of their constituents, use every means in their power to promote its passing during the next session of Parliament."

The resolution was carried unanimously as were the following:—

"That . . . this meeting resolve to urge the factory workers in every mill, in every town, and in every district, to prepare petitions without delay, and forward them to Parliament, praying for the passing of the Ten Hours' Bill. . . ."

"That with a view to supporting Mr. Fielden to carry his Bill, and of laying before the members of Parliament the real wants and wishes of the factory workers, this meeting thinks it desirable that each County should appoint and send to London delegates whose duties shall be to advocate the passing of his Bill, as the only measure nothing short of which will satisfy the factory workers."

h) DELEGATES IN LONDON, 1847

On Wednesday morning a number of delegates from the manufacturing districts of Lancashire and Yorkshire reached London for the purpose of promoting the bill now before Parliament. The . . . Delegates assembled in the evening. . . . The following resolution was unanimously adopted:—"That we the delegates now assembled steadfastly to prosecute the passing of an efficient Ten Hours' Bill for all children and minors employed in factories, record it as our unanimous opinion that nothing short of an efficient Ten Hours' Bill will satisfy our constituents. . . ."

i) THE TEN HOURS' ACT, 1848

After more than thrity years' struggle, the Ten Hours' Bill at last received the sanction of the Legislature in the last Session of the late Parliament. No single Act of modern times was preceded by such ample and full discussion. Public meetings by the thousand were held upon the subject and numerous pamphlets were issued, and the newspaper press was almost constantly debating it. Four select Parliamentary Committees investigated and reported, and the question was the theme of discussion in almost every successive session of every Parliament during that long period. At length, in spite of the most powerful opposition, the advocates of the measure had the gratification of seeing the "Bill" become an "Act" and looked forward to the first of next May, when the ten hour clause is to come into operation. . . . But it appears that the determined opponents of the measure are resolved to make yet another fight against its introduction, and to endeavour to prevail upon Parliament . . . to repeal the ten hour clause before it can come into operation. . . . They have formed a "Millowners' Association" but this association does not take upon itself the task of soliciting a repeal of the law. That is to be done by the factory operators themselves for whose signature the Associated Millowners have prepared a petition. . . . If the Operatives were to aid, in the slightest degree, this movement, they would merely be playing into the hands of a few selfish and greedy speculators. . . . This movement of Associated Millowners demands an immediate counter movement from the Short Time Committees throughout the country. . . .

65. WOMEN AND CHILDREN IN MINES

From the *British Statesman*, July 30th, 1842, describing the
final stages of the Mines and Collieries Act, 1842. This Act
prohibited the labour of women, and of children under ten,
and introduced certain, inadequate, measures of inspection.

. . . LORD BROUGHAM inculcated great caution in the
application of the principles of interfering with the rights
of labour. He admitted that the legislature might interfere with the employment of children in occupations
injurious to their constitutions, but was jealous of interference with the occupation of adults, as the principle
adopted in the present bill might be extended to other
occupations, such as that of pin and needle making etc.
. . . The Marquess of Londonderry hailed the support of
Lord Brougham in opposition to the bill . . . he moved
that the bill be referred to a select Committee. . . .

. . . Lord Skelmersdale moved that women above
40 years of age at present working in collieries should
still be permitted to do so. After considerable discussion,
this was rejected, by 29 to 15. . . .

The Earl of Monteashel proposed to raise the limitation
age of children from ten to twelve years. This was
negatived without a division. . . .

Sources of extracts: *a*) *The Life and Struggles of William Lovett*, 1876, p. 40, describes an early co-op. *b*) A Memorandum by Lovett in the Place Papers (Add. MSS. 27,791, p. 243) illustrates Owen's early opposition to the co-operatives as mere trading associations, far removed in their purpose from his Utopian objectives, although they were in fact an attempt at a practical application of his principles. *c*) The *Northern Star*, January 17th, 1847, reports the second anniversary meeting of the Rochdale Society of Equitable Pioneers, formed December, 1844, and regarded as founders of the modern form of co-operative trading.

a) THE EARLY CO-OPERATIVE SOCIETIES, 1828–9

. . . I WAS induced to join the First London Co-operative Trading Association; a society first established in the premises of the Co-operative Society, Red Lion Square, and subsequently removed to Jerusalem Passage, Clerkenwell. I think it was about the close of the year 1828 that the first of those trading associations was established at Brighton, by a person of the name of Bryan; and its success was such that between four and five hundred similar associations were very soon established in different parts of the country. The members of those societies subscribed a small weekly sum for the raising of a common fund, with which they opened a general store, containing such articles of food, clothing, books, etc., as were most in request among working men; the profits of which were added to the common stock.

As their funds increased some of them employed their members; such as shoemakers, tailors and other domestic trades: paying them journeymen's wages, and adding the profits to their funds. Many of them were also enabled by these means to raise sufficient capital to commence manufactures on a small scale; such as broadcloths, silk, linen, and worsted goods, shoes, hats, cutlery, furniture, etc. Some few months after I had given up my shop in May's

Buildings, I was induced to accept the situation of store-keeper to the "First London Association," the late store-keeper, Mr. James Watson, having resigned.

b) ROBERT OWEN AND THE CO-OPERATIVE SOCIETIES

"The British Association for Promoting Co-operative Knowledge" . . . was formed on the 11th May, 1829, principally by a number of persons who belonged to a Society in Red Lion Square called "the London Co-operative Trading Association." It was intended to accumulate a capital for co-operative purposes by dealing among themselves and acquaintances and thus saving the profit of the retail traders. . . . The persons who took the lead in this affair were James Watson, William Lovett, John Cleave . . . all working men. They had read and admired the writing of Robert Owen . . . and resolved to be instrumental . . . in spreading a knowledge of these works throughout the country. . . . The persons before named . . . during Mr. Owen's visit to N. America resolved to take up such parts of his system as they believed would be appreciated by the working classes. . . . They expected when those who associated having experienced the advantages of these parts of Mr. Owen's system, they might be induced to investigate the whole. . . . As affording some proof in favour of the policy . . . especially the pains taken to impress the working people with the importance of trading associations, in less than six months . . . they had been the means of forming upwards of two hundred of these associations extending from one end of the country to another. . . .

These Societies had not been more than twelve months in existence when Mr. Owen returned from America, when he at once condemned them as altogether opposed to his system, and it was not until he returned from a visit to Manchester, at a delegate meeting, that he could be induced to acknowledge their importance. . . .

July 26th, 1835.

c) THE ROCHDALE PIONEERS

On Tuesday evening the 12th inst. the co-operators and their friends held a public tea in the Bethel preaching rooms in celebration of the second anniversary of the Society. . . .

The secretary . . . congratulated them on the prosperity of the Society; and said the Society consisted of about 110 members, and had at present a capital of £250. The Society neither gave nor received credit . . . the discount for cash paid by the Society for the last quarter, amounted to £13. 2*s*. which had more than paid all expenses of rent, taxes and wages for the same time; the store only being open at certain stated hours each day. The next rule in their Society . . . related to the division of profits, which he recommended them to maintain. He said the mode of dividing the profits was, that on all invested capital 5 per cent. per annum was first paid, the remainder was divided, or formed deposits according as each member had traded with the Society. There had been £30 disposed of in the latter way, on the trade of the quarter just ended. By the above arrangement two important results had been obtained—it often happened that persons with large families had but little spare capital with much trade; and those with no, or but small families, had more spare money with less trade, and therefore the above rule benefited both parties, one by having good interest for their money, and the other by having the profits on their larger trade. Capital did not claim all, neither ought it, and it appeared to him whenever it did, the poorer members ceased to have an interest in the Society— a fact which had been proved by experience. . . .

Part Seven

THE STRUGGLE FOR FREE THOUGHT

67. RICHARD CARLILE'S TRIAL FOR BLASPHEMY, 1819

Pioneer in the struggle for freedom of thought, Richard Carlile made his small shop in Fleet Street for many years the centre of the agitation which ultimately broke the ban on "heretical" writings, and won an unstamped Press. Like many of the others in this struggle, he was printer, publisher and bookseller in one. Not only was he himself imprisoned for his activities (for terms totalling nine years and three months), but so also were his heroic wife and 150 of his "shopmen." The document below refers to his trial for publishing the rationalist and Radical writings of Tom Paine. Carlile quoted the whole of Paine's *Age of Reason* in his defence, so that the banned book formed part of the official proceedings of the trial. The extract is from his own paper, the *Republican*, December 17th, 1819.

RICHARD CARLILE . . . saith that this information was filed . . . against this deponent . . . charging him with, having maliciously published a blasphemous libel, entitled the Theological Works of Thomas Paine. . . . That deponent verily believes the proceedings in the course of the trial were irregular, and not according to law and that the verdict . . . of guilty, was hereby contaminated.

And saith, that deponent . . . protested against the authority of this court to try the charge of blasphemy, . . . there being no person defamed, which deponent believe to be necessary to support the charge of libel . . . and saith, that the strongest charge in the aforesaid information was, that this deponent had incurred "the high displeasure of Almighty God" no proof of which was offered to the court or jury. . . .

And saith, that during this trial this court was twice adjourned . . . and that the jurors did separate, without the consent of this deponent, which was contrary to the laws of this country, and to the great injury of this deponent. . . .

And saith, that deponent in the course of his trial was prevented by the undue interposition of the Lord Chief

P

Justice, in making his defence, and proving to the jury, that this deponent's intention was good (and not wicked and malicious as charged . . .) by shewing the truth and moral tendency of the book . . . published. . . .

And saith, that this deponent had subpœnaed several eminent men, amongst others the Archbishop of Canterbury, the High Priest of the Jews and the Astronomer Royal, with the most eminent men in each Christian Sect, to shew to the jury, that christianity could not be part of the law of the land, as christianity could not possibly be defined and that no man could possibly say what it really was, without finding his opinions opposed by some other person. And that the Lord Chief Justice . . . denied this deponent the benefit of these important evidences. . . . And further saith . . . when the jury . . . did send into Court requesting that two statutes . . . should be sent to them, . . . before his lordship allowed them to see the statutes required . . . [he] renewed his address to them for several minutes, which deponent verily believes was to his great injury. . . .

RICHARD CARLILE.

Sworn in Open Court.
this 9th day of November 1819.

68. JAMES WATSON'S MEMORIES

James Watson (1799–1874), a Yorkshireman, was a colleague of Lovett and Hetherington. Beginning his working life as a Leeds drysalter's apprentice, he became one of the most active Radical printers and publishers in the London movement. The extract is from *James Watson: A Memoir*, by W. J. Linton, 1879, pp. 14–19.

I LIVED with my mother and sister; but not liking to be a burthen to them . . . resolved to quit our native town and seek employment . . . in Leeds. . . . I found employment at a drysalter's as warehouseman, and had the charge of a saddle horse.

It was in the autumn of 1818 that I first became acquainted with politics and theology. Passing along Briggate one evening, I saw . . . a bill, which stated that the Radical Reformers held their meetings in a room in that court. Curiosity prompted me to go and hear what was going on. I found them reading Wooler's *Black Dwarf*, Carlile's *Republican* and Cobbett's *Register*. I remembered my mother being in the habit of reading Cobbett's *Register*, and saying she "wondered people spoke so much against it; she saw nothing bad in it." After hearing it read in the meeting room, I was of my mother's opinion.

. . . From this time until 1822 I was actively engaged . . . in collecting subscriptions for Mr. Carlile, spreading the liberal and free thinking literature and, by meetings and discussions, endeavouring to obtain the right of free discussion. In 1821 the Government renewed the prosecutions for blasphemy and Mr. Carlile (then in Dorchester gaol . . .) appealed to the friends in the country to serve in the shop. . . . On the 18th September 1822 I arrived in London. . . . I served in the shop at 5 Water Lane, Fleet Street. . . . At this time the plan of selling the books by a sort of clockwork, so that the seller was not seen, was in practice. . . . Towards the end of February I was arrested for selling a copy of Palmer's *Principles of Nature*

. . . sent to Clerkenwell Prison, where I remained six weeks. . . . My trial took place on the 23rd April. . . . I was convicted, and sentenced to twelve months' imprisonment in Coldbaths-Fields prison, and to find bail for my good behaviour for two years. . . . I endeavoured to make the best use of the opportunity for study and investigation. . . . I was liberated on 24th April 1824. . . . I applied for employment at a number of places, but found my having been in prison, and shopman to Mr. Carlile, a formidable difficulty, and I incurred in consequence considerable privation. . . .

At the end of 1825 I learned the art of a compositor. . . . In 1825 I was first introduced to the advocates of Mr. Owen's New View of Society; and to the end of 1829 I was actively engaged helping to form co-operative associations and societies for political and religious liberty. . . . In May [1830] I . . . commenced the business of bookseller. . . . In 1831 I became a printer and publisher. . . . At this time I became a member of the National Union of Working Classes. . . .

In February 1833 I was summoned to Bow Street for selling a *Poor Man's Guardian* . . . the magistrates . . . considered me as bad as . . . Hetherington and sentenced me to six months in the same Clerkenwell Prison. . . . I was liberated on the 29th July, and attended the same day a meeting to commemorate the third anniversary of the French revolution. . . .

69. HENRY HETHERINGTON AND THE "UNSTAMPED"

Henry Hetherington (1792–1849), master printer and publisher, was apprenticed in his youth to Hansard. He became the outstanding figure in the struggle for a cheap and free Press, and was one of the group responsible for framing the People's Charter. After the first great period of Chartism in 1838–9, he devoted himself mainly to free-thought agitation. The account of Hetherington is quoted below from Lovett, *op. cit.*, p. 59, and includes the names of other pioneers. See also Nos. 9, 33, 73.

In 1830 I became connected with the "Unstamped Agitation" one of the most important political movements that I was ever associated with. This unstamped warfare had its commencement in the publication of *The Poor Man's Guardian*, by Mr. Henry Hetherington; although the idea of publishing a substitute for a newspaper, in such a manner as to evade Castlereagh's Act, first originated with Mr. William Carpenter. This last gentleman, a well-known author and editor who has been connected with most of the political movements of the last twenty years or more, believed that he could evade this infamous Act (the 38th of Geo. III, etc., passed to put down Mr. Cobbett's two-penny publications) by issuing weekly what he called his Political Letters. Before, however, any of these were published, Mr. Hetherington brought out a series of *Penny Daily Papers*, in a letter form, addressed to different individuals with the view of evading the Act of Parliament, and at the same time to provide cheap political information for the people. After a short time, however, they were published weekly, each having a title of a *Penny Paper for the People, by the Poor Man's Guardian*; and after Mr. Hetherington's first conviction he changed the title to the *Poor Man's Guardian, Published in Defiance of Law to try the Power of Right against Might*. This publication was first edited by Mr. Mayhew, a brother,

I believe, of the author of *London Labour and the Poor*, and subsequently by Mr. James Bronterre O'Brien, a writer and politician of some celebrity.

It was not started long, however, before the Stamp Office authorities commenced a fierce warfare against it, first against the publisher, and then against the booksellers who sold it. This having deterred many from selling it, caused some few of us to volunteer the supplying of it to persons at their own houses within any reasonable distance; and subsequently to organise a general fund for the support of those who were suffering or likely to suffer for striving to disseminate cheap political information amongst the people. This fund was called the "Victim Fund"; it was kept up by small weekly subscriptions during the many years the contest lasted, and contributed in no small degree to the success of that contest. The Committee of Management consisted for the most part of Messrs. Cleave, Watson, Warden, Russell, Petrie, Mansell and Devonshire Saul: Julian Hibbert was our treasurer; I was the sub-treasurer, and acted also as secretary during the greater part of the time and Mr. Russell the remaining portion. We met weekly in an upstair room at the Hope Coffee House, King Street, Smithfield, then kept by Mr. John Cleave, and subsequently at his house in Shoe Lane. Finding that the booksellers refused to sell the *Poor Man's Guardian*, and some few other Radical publications subsequently started, we advertised for persons to sell them in the streets and from house to house, and met with many volunteers; some of them from a sincere desire to serve the cause, and others for the mere trifling benefit we held out to them, which was generally a stock of papers to begin with, and a pound in money for every month (or shorter time) they might suffer imprisonment. . . .

Mr. Hetherington . . . was not the kind of character to yield. . . . The first time he appeared at Bow Street to answer to the charge of printing and publishing the *Guardian* and *Republican* he honestly told the magistrates that he was determined to resist the efforts of a corrupt government to suppress the voice of the people. His conviction having been confirmed at the next session, he in the interim set off for a tour through the country, and was greatly instrumental in calling up the spirit of the people in opposition to the persecution the Whigs were then waging against the Press. Finding also that many of the old established booksellers were fearful of selling his publications, he and his friends succeeded in inducing many other persons to commence the sale of them. Many of those were prosecuted and imprisoned; but such proceedings only served to enlist public sympathy in their favour, and to increase their business; many of whom are now the largest booksellers for cheap literature in the kingdom. In this tour the police pursued Mr. Hetherington in all directions. . . .

The contest lasted upwards of five years; during which time upwards of 500 persons in different parts of the kingdom suffered imprisonment for the publication, or sale, of the *Poor Man's Guardian*, the *Political Letters*, the *Republican*, the *Police Gazette*, and other Radical publications. Among those persons, Mr. Wm. Carpenter was imprisoned six months in King's Bench Prison; Mr. Henry Hetherington was imprisoned three times: twice in Clerkenwell Prison, for six months each time, and in King's Bench for twelve months. Mr. James Watson was imprisoned twice in Clerkenwell Prison, for six months each time; Mr. John Cleave, for two months in Tothill Fields Prison; and in the City Prison till a fine inflicted on him was paid; together with the seizure of his printing press and printing materials. Mr. Abel Heywood, of Manchester, was imprisoned three months; Mrs. Mann, of Leeds, three months, and several others. None of the victims being allowed trial by jury, but merely condemned in a summary manner by the magistrates; the police being mostly the witnesses, and Mr. Timms, from the Stamp Office, the prosecutor. And what adds to the monstrous injustice of this Government persecution is the fact that, after so many hundred persons had been fined and imprisoned for selling the *Poor Man's Guardian*, it was finally declared before Lord Lyndhurst and a special jury, to be a strictly legal publication.

This warfare, however, eventually created a public opinion sufficiently powerful to cause the Government to give up the *fourpenny stamp* upon newspapers, and to substitute a *penny stamp* instead. But this triumphant change was by no means so important as the amount of good that otherwise resulted from the contest. For the unstamped publications may be said *to have originated the cheap literature of the present day*—for few publications existed before they commenced—and the beneficial effects of this cheap literature on the minds and morals of our population are beyond all calculation.

70. SELLING THE "UNSTAMPED"

From the *Poor Man's Guardian*, November 12th, 1831.

THE following account of a conviction which took place at the Court-room, Stockport, on Thursday, the 27th October, before Captain Clarke and other magistrates, has been transmitted by a friend.—JOSEPH SWANN for selling the *Poor Man's Guardian*, *Hunt's Address*, Unstamped Almanacks, and other Publications . . . on Thursday last . . . was asked what he had to say in his defence.

DEFENDANT: Well, Sir, I have been out of employment for some time, neither can I obtain work; my family are all starving; I have applied for relief from the Overseers, but am denied it, and I am glad to sell anything for a living. And for another reason, the weightiest of all, I sell them for the good of my fellow countrymen; to let them see how they are misrepresented in Parliament, and to shew them how they may become more fairly represented, for I think it unjust that men shall be compelled to obey those laws which they have not a voice in framing. It is the *right* of every man to be allowed to sanction every law by which they are led, and I wish to let the people know how they are humbugged.

BENCH: Why do you hawk unstamped Almanacks?

DEFENDANT: Because I have had no voice in stamping them, and no man ought to be governed by laws which he has not previously approved of.

BENCH: Hold your tongue a moment.

DEFENDANT: I shall not! for I wish every man to read those publications (pointing to the *Poor Man's Guardian*, *Hunt's Letters*, etc.).

BENCH: You are very insolent, therefore you are committed to three months' imprisonment in Knutsford House of Correction, to hard labor.

DEFENDANT: I've nothing to thank you for; and whenever I come out, I'll hawk them again. And *mind you*, the first that I hawk shall be to your house (looking at Captain Clarke).

BENCH: Stand down.

DEFENDANT: No! I shall not stand down for *you*.

He was then *forcibly* removed from the dock and back to the New Bailey.

It was must be borne in mind that J. Swann is the very identical man who suffered four and a half years in Chester Castle for selling *The Republican* (Mr. Carlile's) some few years ago.

71. THE VALUE OF A WORKING-CLASS PRESS

From the *Northern Star*, March 24th, 1838. By Bronterre O'Brien.

WITHOUT a London daily paper we can do nothing effectual for the people. I have often expressed to you that opinion and every succeeding day's experience confirms me in it. If there is to be a revolution in this country (and I maintain there must be one) it is the duty of the people's friends to achieve it at the least possible cost of violence, tribulation and suffering, to all classes. In other words, it is our duty to render the revolution which now menaces society—a revolution of order, enlightenment and permanent benefit. To accomplish such a revolution to distinguish it from all former revolutions we must have an *instructed* as well as a united people. . . .

72. G. J. HOLYOAKE IN PRISON FOR BLASPHEMY, 1842

From *Sixty Years of an Agitator's Life*, by G. J. Holyoake, 1906, Chapter 31. For Holyoake, see No. 43.

BEFORE long the magistrates . . . called upon me to wear the prison dress. My answer was that "I did not wish to do it," . . . as I was no criminal it would be admitting it to wear the dress of crime by my own choice. In gaol I knew official force must be supreme; therefore, I never said "I would not" do a thing, only that "I did not wish to do it." Of course they said they should compel me. In that case my reply was "it would be necessary to dress me every morning, as I might not like to put the dress on myself." . . . It was never done. . . .

Another trouble soon arose. When the prayer bell rang the first morning, all the prisoners filed out to chapel, but I remained. Seeing my allotted place vacant, the chaplain sent the gaoler for me. I said "it was incredible that the chaplain should send for me. He knew my imprisonment was owing to my not properly believing in his ministration, and my voluntary attendance at his chapel would be hypocrisy in me." The gaoler said "he must carry out his instructions and take me there." My reply was, "in that case you had better get assistance and carry me, as I do not think I should like to go. Whether the chaplain's congregation will be edified by seeing a dissentient worshipper carried into chapel every morning it will be for him to decide." Probably the gaoler concluded that this mode of bringing me to church needed special instructions—he went to seek them, and returned to me no more.

73. LAST WILL AND TESTAMENT OF HENRY HETHERINGTON, 1849

From *Life and Character of Henry Hetherington*, edited by G. J. Holyoake, 1849. For Hetherington, see, above, Nos. 9, 33, 69.

As life is uncertain, it behoves everyone to make preparations for death; I deem it therefore a duty incumbent on me, ere I quit this life, to express in writing, for the satisfaction and guidance of esteemed friends, my feelings and opinions in reference to our common principles. . . .

In the first place, then—I calmly and deliberately declare that I do not believe in the popular notion of the existence of an Almighty, All-wise and Benevolent God—possessing intelligence, and conscious of His own operations; because these attributes involve such a mass of absurdities and contradictions, so much cruelty and injustice on His part to the poor and destitute portion of His creatures—that, in my opinion, no rational reflecting mind can, after disinterested investigation, give credence to the existence of such a Being.

[In the] second [place] I believe death to be an eternal sleep—that I shall never live again in this world, or another, with a consciousness that I am the same identical person that once lived, performed the duties, and exercised the functions of a human being.

[In the] third [place] I consider priestcraft and superstition the greatest obstacle to human improvement and happiness. During my life I have, to the best of my ability, sincerely and strenuously exposed and opposed them, and die with a firm conviction that Truth, Justice, and Liberty will never be permanently established on earth till every vestige of priestcraft and superstition shall be utterly destroyed.

[In the] fourth [place], I have ever considered that the only religion useful to man consists exclusively of the practice of morality, and in the mutual interchange of kind actions. In such a religion there is no room for priests—and when I see them interfering at our births, marriages, and deaths, pretending to conduct us safely through this state of being to another and happier world, any disinterested person of the least shrewdness and discernment must perceive that their sole aim is to stultify the minds of the people by their incomprehensible doctrines, that they may the more effectually fleece the poor deluded sheep who listen to their empty babblings and mystifications.

[In the] fifth [place], as I have lived so I die, a determined opponent to their nefarious and plundering system. I wish my friends, therefore, to deposit my remains in unconsecrated ground, and trust they will allow no priest, or clergyman of any denomination, to interfere in any way whatever at my funeral. My earnest desire is, that no relation or friend shall wear black or any kind of mourning, as I consider it contrary to our rational principles to indicate respect for a departed friend by complying with a hypocritical custom. . . .

These are my views and feelings in quitting an existence that has been chequered with the plagues and pleasures of a competitive, scrambling, selfish system; a system by which the moral and social aspirations of the noblest human being are nullified by incessant toil and physical deprivations; by which, indeed, all men are trained to be either slaves, hypocrites, or criminals. Hence my ardent attachment to the principles of that great and good man —ROBERT OWEN. I quit this world with a firm conviction that his system is the only true road to human emancipation; that it is, indeed, the only just system for regulating the affairs of honest, intelligent human beings—the only one yet made known to the world, that is based on truth, justice and equality. While the land, machines, tools, implements of production, and the produce of man's toil, are exclusively in possession of the do-nothings; and labour is the sole possession of the wealth-producers—a marketable commodity, bought up and directed by wealthy idlers—never-ending misery must be their inevitable lot.

Robert Owen's system, if rightly understood and faithfully carried out, rectifies all these anomalies. It makes man the proprietor of his own labour and of the elements of production—it places him in a condition to enjoy the entire fruits of his labour and surrounds him with circumstances that will make him intelligent, rational and happy. Grateful to Mr. Owen for the happiness I have experienced in contemplating the superiority of his system, I could not die happy without recommending my fellow-countrymen to study its principles and earnestly strive to establish them in practice. . . .

I have indefatigably, sincerely and disinterestedly laboured to improve the condition of humanity—believing it to be the duty of every man to leave the world better than he found it; and if I have not pursued this object with that wisdom and discretion that should mark at all times the conduct of a rational man, I have zealously maintained what appeared to me to be right, and paid the penalty of what my opponents may term my indiscretions in many cruel persecutions. I freely forgive all who have injured me in the struggle; and die in the hope and consolation that a time is approaching when the spirit of antagonism will give place to fraternal affection and universal co-operation to promote the happiness of mankind.

(Signed) HENRY HETHERINGTON.
Witnessed by George Jacob Holyoake, Henry Allsop Ivory, John Kenny. *Aug. 21, 1849.*

Part Eight

INTERNATIONALISM IN THE BRITISH WORKING-CLASS MOVEMENT

74. WAR AND THE WORKING CLASS

By Bronterre O'Brien, *Operative*, November 4th, 1838,
referring to the Napoleonic Wars (No. 1).

THE aristocrats and usurers of the two nations succeeded
in getting up the WAR . . . need we say that it cost the
two nations and Europe generally the loss of several
millions of human lives and added upwards of 500 million
sterling to our "national debt" . . . to the unrepresented
classes they have read a lesson which we know will never
be forgotten. They have taught us to regard all wars with
horror, which are got up only to subserve the interests of
the upper and middle orders. Hereafter, if we go to war,
it shall be only for national purposes. "No more fighting
for Kings and aristocrats; no more wars to put down
democracy in France or elsewhere! No more waste of
blood and treasure to suppress democratic principles in
England; no more human sacrifice to Mars, Mammon,
or Moloch for the sake of enabling tyrants to ride rough-
shod over the largest and best part of the human race."

75. THE BRITISH WORKERS ADDRESS THE IRISH

The following article by Bronterre O'Brien refers to an "Address by the Radical Reformers of England, Scotland and Wales to the Irish People," which was signed by representatives of one hundred and thirty-six Chartist and workers' associations all over the country—a truly impressive demonstration of sympathy with the plight of the Irish people, who were regarded by the Chartists as victims, like themselves, of the same ruling classes. From the *Operative*, November 4th, 1838.

MOST urgently do we implore, most ardently do we hope that our Irish brethren will grasp with the generous warmth inherent in their character, the hand of fellowship thus tendered to them. . . . A holy alliance between the oppressed of the two countries is not more essential to the interests of the one than it is to those of the other. Ireland has never before had such an opportunity of righting herself. For the first time in her political history she is offered the assistance of England, Scotland and Wales, in the recovery of her long-lost rights, and the offer is made by the heads of political bodies, who may be fairly said to represent nine tenths of the British population. . . .

Ireland has no possible means of extricating herself from the frightful state of destitution and bondage in which her oppressors hold her, without the assistance of the men of Great Britain. The converse of this proposition applies with almost equal force to the impoverished people of England and Scotland. An immense portion of the agricultural wealth of Ireland is annually drained into this country to enrich bands of absentee landlords, fund lords, and usurers of every description who give the agriculturists of Ireland not one shilling's worth of value in return. Again; an immense portion of the manufactured wealth of England and Scotland is, in like manner, annually drained into Ireland to enrich the squirearchy, shopocracy, law—church, Government agents, military and constabulary officers, and, above all, the hordes of corn factors, butter merchants, cattle dealers, jobbers, and contractors of all sorts that overspread that country, and who yield the operatives of England and Ireland not one shilling's worth of value in return for the manufactured produce absorbed by them. . . .

Well then, seeing that the productive classes of the two islands have the same wants and the same enemies; why should they not look forward to the same remedy, and make common cause against the common oppressor? . . . How? . . . By a grand alliance between the oppressed or unrepresented classes of Ireland, with the oppressed or unrepresented classes of Great Britain. . . . When? As soon as Ireland's co-operation has been verified by the appearance of one million of Irish signatures to the National Petition. . . .

76. INTERNATIONAL WORKING CLASS UNITY

Speech of G. J. Harney to the German Democratic Society for the Education of the Working Classes, from the *Northern Star*, February 14th, 1846. George Julian Harney (1817–97), an agitator from his youth, early became a militant Chartist leader. He served a prison sentence for selling unstamped periodicals before he was twenty, and was Editor of the *Northern Star*, 1843–50. One of the most internationally active of the Chartists, he was the moving spirit of the Society of Fraternal Democrats, in which organisation he first came into active contact with Marx and Engels, with whom he remained in touch throughout their lives. See also Nos. 51, 78, 79, 80, and, for his greeting to the Dock Strike, in 1889, Vol. III of this series.

NATIONALITY has in other times been necessary; it saved mankind from universal and irredeemable slavery. In our day, too, the invoking of the spirit of nationality in some countries is indispensable to rekindle life in those countries. . . . However, we must have no king Czartoryski. We must have no kingdom of Italy such as the Italian deputies solicited of the Holy Alliance in 1815. We must have the sovereignty of the people in both countries, the education of the people in both countries. The education of the people, and at least, the progressive social advance of the people, ever progressing, until the people own no masters but themselves, and enjoy the fruits of their labour, uninfluenced by oppressors in any shape or name. In other countries, such as England and France, there is no need to rekindle national feelings; on the contrary, the efforts of the good men in both countries should be directed to the abolition of the remaining prejudices which a barbarous cultivation of the spirit of nationality, in days gone by, called into existence.

I appeal to the oppressed classes of every land . . . to unite . . . for the triumph of the common cause. "Divide and conquer" has been the motto of oppressors; "Unite and triumph!" should be our counter-motto. Whatever national differences divide Poles, Russians, Prussians, Hungarians and Italians, these national differences have not prevented the Russian, Austrian and Prussian despots uniting together to maintain their tyranny. Why, then, cannot the people of those countries unite for the obtainment of their liberty? . . .

The cause of the people in all countries is the same— the cause of labour, enslaved and plundered labour. . . . In each country the tyranny of the few and the slavery of the many are variously developed, but the principle in all is the same. . . . In all countries the men who grow the wheat live on potatoes. The men who rear the cattle do not taste flesh food. The men who cultivate the vine have only the dregs of its noble juice. The men who make the clothing are in rags. The men who build the houses live in hovels. The men who create every necessity, comfort and luxury, are steeped in misery. Working men of all nations, are not your grievances, your wrongs, the same? Is not your good cause, then, one and the same also? We may differ as to the means, or different circumstances may render different means necessary, but the great end— the veritable emancipation of the human race—must be the one aim and end of all. . . . May the working classes of all nations combine in brotherhood for the triumph of their common cause.

77. THE GERMAN DEMOCRATIC COMMUNISTS
OF BRUSSELS
TO MR. FEARGUS O'CONNOR, 1846

From the *Northern Star*, July 25th, 1846. O'Connor opposed
Sir John Cam Hobhouse, a Whig Minister (see No. 8*d*),
at a by-election, won at the hustings, but was defeated
at the poll. See note to No. 45.

WE embrace the occasion of your splendid success at the
Nottingham election to congratulate you, and through
you the English Chartists, on this signal victory. We consider the defeat of a Free Trade minister at the show of
hands by an enormous Chartist majority, and at the very
time too that Free Trade principles are triumphant in
the legislature . . . as a sign that the working classes of
England are very well aware of the position they have to
take after the triumph of Free Trade . . . that now the
great struggle of capital and labour, of *bourgeois* and
proletarian, must come to a decision. The ground is now
cleared by the retreat of the landed aristocracy from the
contest; middle class and working class are the only
classes betwixt whom there can be a possible struggle.

The contending parties have their respective battle
cries forced upon them by their interests and mutual
position: the middle class—"extension of commerce by
any means whatsoever, and a Ministry of Lancashire
cotton lords to carry this out": the working class—
"A democratic reconstruction of the Constitution upon
the basis of the People's Charter," by which the working
class will become the ruling class of England. We rejoice
to see the English working men fully aware of this altered
state of parties; of the new period Chartist agitation has
entered into; with the final defeat of the third party, the
aristocracy; of the prominent position which Chartism
henceforth will and must occupy, in pite of the "conspiracy of silence" of the middle class press; and finally,
of the new task, which by these new circumstances has

devolved upon them. That they are quite aware of the task is proved by their intention *to go to the poll* at the next general election. . . .

We hesitate not a moment in declaring that the *Star* is the only English newspaper . . . which is free from national and religious prejudice; which sympathises with the democrats and working men . . . all over the world; which in all these points speaks the mind of the English working class. . . . We hereby declare that we shall do everything in our power to extend the circulation of the *Northern Star* on the continent, and to have extracts from it translated in as many continental papers as possible. . . .

ENGELS.

PH. GIGOT.

MARX.

Brussels, July 17th, 1846.

78. BRITISH FOREIGN POLICY

From an election address of G. J. Harney, at Tiverton, July 20th, 1847. Harney opposed Lord Palmerston, who held the seat. *Northern Star*, July 24th, 1847. For Harney, see No. 76.

THE foreign policy of the present administration has been ruinous to the cause of freedom, and disgraceful to the character of this country. By basely crouching before the confiscators of Cracow, and trampling upon the independence of Portugal, Lord Palmerston (one of your present members) . . . successfully laboured to win for England . . . the hatred of the oppressed of every land. . . . Repudiating the views of the advocates of "permanent and universal peace," which in the present state of the world I think visionary and impracticable, I would nevertheless oppose all wars and "interventions" except those which the voice of the people might pronounce absolutely indispensable for self defence, or the protection of the weak against the powerful. I would labour to put an end to the alliance of this country with despotic governments; and I should consider it my bounden duty to urge the claims of the people of Poland, with the view of promoting the speedy restoration of the nationality and freedom of that cruelly persecuted and long suffering race. . . .

79. KARL MARX TO THE SOCIETY OF FRATERNAL DEMOCRATS, 1847

Speech of Karl Marx to the Society of Fraternal Democrats; from the *Northern Star*, December 4th, 1847. The Society was formed in September, 1845, to unite the democrats of various countries living in London, and provide them a platform on which they could associate for common ends with British workers' leaders. (See No. 76.) Marx was in London for the Second Congress of the Communist League, which commissioned him to write the *Communist Manifesto*, published in London, March, 1848.

THE anniversary of the Polish insurrection of 1830 was celebrated on . . . the 29th November by a public meeting . . . called by the Society of Fraternal Democrats. . . . Citizen Schapper . . . read the following document:

"To the members of the society of Fraternal Democrats Assembling in London.

"We, the undersigned members of the committee of the Democratic Society, established at Brussels, for advancing the Union and Fraternity of all Nations, have the honour to delegate to you, Dr. Charles Marx, vice-president of this committee, for the purpose of establishing relations of correspondence and sympathy between the two societies. M. Marx has full power to act in the name of this committee for the purpose above mentioned." . . .

Dr. Marx, the delegate from Brussels, then came forward and was greeted with every demonstration of welcome, and delivered an energetic oration in the German language, the substance of which was as follows:—

He had been sent by the Democrats of Brussels to speak in their name to the Democrats of London, and through them to the Democrats of Britain, to call on them to cause to be holden a congress of nations—a congress of working men to establish liberty all over the world. The middle class, the Free Traders, had held a congress, but their fraternity was a one-sided one, and the moment they found that such congresses were likely to benefit working men, that moment the fraternity would cease, and their congresses be dissolved. The Democrats of Belgium felt that the Chartists of England were the real Democrats, and that the moment they carried the six points of their Charter, the road to liberty would be opened to the whole world. "Effect this grand object, then, you working men of England," said the speaker, "and you will be hailed as the saviours of the whole human race."

80. THE REVOLUTION IN FRANCE, 1848

a) An Address to the People of Paris, adopted by the Executive Committee of the National Charter Association, by the Fraternal Democrats, by the Metropolitan Delegate Committee of the Chartists of London and by a great public meeting of Chartist working men of London. From the *Northern Star*, March 4th, 1848.

HEROIC CITIZENS,—

The thunder notes of your victory have sounded across the Channel, awakening the sympathies and hopes of every lover of liberty. We hasten to express to you our congratulations, and to thank you for the glorious service you have rendered to the human race.

By your courage and magnanimity, your heroism and devotion to principle, you have consecrated right of insurrection; the last resource of the oppressed—the last argument against oppression.

You have hurled from power a cruel, corrupt, and tyrannical government; you have punished a perfidious King for his black treason to the principles which he pretended to adopt when placed at the head of the French nation in 1830; you have exhibited a spectacle of unparalleled heroism, and thereby set an example to all the enslaved nations of the earth.

Honour to those noble soldiers who refused to turn their arms against the people! . . . The fire that consumed the Throne of the royal traitor and tyrant will kindle the torch of liberty in every country of Europe. . . .

You are the advanced guard of Freedom's army, and we can assure you that the British people will never sanction a fratricidal war against their brethren in France. . . .

b) Report of the Delegation to Paris, 1848. From the *Northern Star*, March 11th. 1848.

THE Executive Committee of the National Charter Association having appointed Philip McGrath, the

Chartists of London Ernest Jones, and the Fraternal Democrats Julian Harney, to bear their congratulatory address to the Provisional Government, the Delegation on reaching Paris . . . proceeded to the Hotel de Ville . . . where . . . they were immediately received by the ministers. . . .

Ernest Jones then addressed (in French) the members of the Government, and said: Citizens, we come as a deputation of the oppressed to the free; not to ask for aid, but to express admiration. To thank you for showing how an enslaved people can liberate themselves; and to tell you that the example of France is not lost upon the heart of England. We too have our Guizot and we will tolerate him, no more than you have done yours. We too have grievances to redress, wounds to heal, and misery to solace. We, too, are determined to achieve our rights, and can read the plainer by the light of your revolution. We come to thank you, in the name of England and the world, and to assure you of the friendship of the British people, which will never permit its government to make war on the French Republic. Should the English and the French stand on the same battlefield, it will not be as foes, but side by side, to re-establish a Poland or restore an Italy. The Speaker then read a French translation of the address; and the original, handsomely mounted and adorned with the tricolour, was placed in the hands of Ledru Rollin by Julian Harney.

. . . The Government then had the Chartist Address hung over the presidential chair in the Hall of Audience —and the news having spread through Paris of the arrival and distinguished reception of the Chartist envoys, the liveliest sympathy was expressed by the people.

. . . The Delegation, in conclusion, are happy to express their conviction that their mission has drawn closer the bonds of fraternity, uniting the *poor* of France with the *enslaved* of England.

THE END

INDEX

Printed in Great Britain by
The Camelot Press Ltd., London and Southampton